POWER NEGOTIATING TACTICS AND TECHNIQUES

Also by the Author

The Miracle of Instant Memory Power

Psychic Advantage: Key to Controlling People and Situations

POWER
NEGOTIATING
TACTICS
AND
TECHNIQUES

David V. Lewis

Prentice-Hall, Inc.

Englewood Cliffs, New Jersey

Prentice-Hall International, Inc., *London*
Prentice-Hall of Australia, Pty. Ltd., *Sydney*
Prentice-Hall Canada, Ltd., *Toronto*
Prentice-Hall of India Private Ltd., *New Delhi*
Prentice-Hall of Japan, Inc., *Tokyo*
Prentice-Hall of Southeast Asia Pte. Ltd., *Singapore*
Whitehall Books, Ltd., *Wellington, New Zealand*

© 1981 *by*

Prentice-Hall, Inc.
Englewood Cliffs, N.J.

Library of Congress Cataloging in Publication Data

Lewis, David V.,
   Power negotiating tactics and techniques.

   Includes index.
   1. Negotiation.   I. Title.
BF637.N4L48   158'.5   81-5164
ISBN 0-13-686808-8   AACR2

Printed in the United States of America

WHAT THIS BOOK
CAN DO FOR YOU

Power negotiating is the ability to change the attitude or behavior of another—to *get your way* when dealing with others.

How frequently do you *get your way?* Unless you're a power negotiator, probably not very often. My observation is that the average person uses only about 25 to 30 percent of his or her negotiating ability. Frequently, far less than that! Why? There are several good reasons.

Overcoming Negotiating "Blocks"

First, negotiation isn't something you normally learn in a classroom. You learn it, for the most part, in the arena of life, often with faulty perception.

Second, you are probably not aware of, and thus haven't fully developed, the personality traits of a successful power negotiator.

Finally, you simply have not been exposed to the proven tactics and techniques used by power negotiators from many walks of life.

That's what this book is all about—helping you develop the personal attributes of a successful negotiator and master the techniques used by lawyers, salespeople, diplomats, labor relations counsellors, agents and other top professionals.

Discussing the Nature of Power

In the first section of this book (Chapters 1 and 2) you'll find out about the true nature of power—who holds it, and *why*. For instance, almost everyone knows that *knowledge* is power. Power negotiators additionally realize—and exploit the fact—that *position, credibility, appearance,* and *information* are among other critical sources of power.

Power negotiators constantly use the psychology of power to their advantage. They constantly out-negotiate others because they realize that: power must be recognized before it exists; it is possible to have power with *no* power at all; and you can gain leverage once you realize what power pressures others will submit to.

How to Increase Your Power Level

You'll discover how to upgrade your power level further by

- Bolstering your self-image, and at the same time, your expectation level.

- Learning to communicate more effectively.

- Mastering the very fine art of making concessions.

It's equally important that you don't *mis*-use power. This is what Chapter 2 is all about—making your negotiations win-win rather than win-lose propositions.

"Certainly it's important to 'win' in negotiation," said Bill Johnson, a successful Oklahoma attorney, "but the real key to successful negotiation is to let the other person get *something* out of the deal."

At a minimum, your opponent should finish with his self-esteem intact. A number of other proven facesavers will be discussed in this chapter.

Using the Negotiating Tactics of the Pros

The second section (Chapters 3 through 9) gets down to brass tacks about negotiating tactics and techniques used by top-notch people in their profession.

These chapters are filled with examples of people who have increased their income, prestige, and popularity by improving their ability to power negotiate.

For example, Bob Grayson, a successful businessman, uses a legitimate deadline ("June 1st is absolutely the last day I'll take bids") to close deals on *his* terms. He also has learned that an *imaginary* deadline can frequently work as well. "It's amazing," he said, "how people will often accept *your* deadline as *theirs*."

You'll find out how other "timing" tactics, such as *patience, fait accompli,* and *surprise* can add to your position as a power negotiator.

How to Negotiate Money and Prices

Negotiating can become sticky indeed when it comes to money and pricing. That's why you'll want to master such tactics as *take-it-or-leave-it, escalation, highballing,* and *price squeezes.*

Though "offensive" tactics are stressed, even the strongest negotiators sometimes need a stout defense, as in war and football, to neutralize dubious tactics such as *lowballing* (car buyers will recognize this one) when used *against* them.

On occasion it's better to let a knowledgeable third party negotiate for you. You'll gain access to the secrets used by outstanding sports and literary agents to land huge contracts for others. And you'll also find how *limited authority,* and in some cases, *no* authority at all, can work to your advantage in power negotiating.

The Secret of Forming Alliances

In still other cases, you can enhance your power negotiating posture by forming strong or complementary alliances. It's a tactic called *association. Disassociation,* the other side of the coin, can be used equally well.

Almost all successful power negotiators know how to exploit *propaganda* to their advantage. Chapter 8 is devoted to proven power tactics such as: making *facts and figures* work for you; finding solid sources of *information,* and using intentional *misunderstanding* and *"ignorance"* to further your ends.

Knowing how to "break off" a negotiation is as important as knowing when to close a sale. Thus Chapter 9 gives details on how power negotiators use a host of closing techniques and tactics, including: *withdrawal, ultimatum, brinksmanship, take-it-or-leave-it,* and *refusal.*

How to Become a Power Negotiator

The final section deals with your ability to become a power negotiator in a variety of social and business situations.

Almost all negotiation is done at two levels, one involving issues, the other having to do with personalities. This is why a true power negotiator *must* develop strong interpersonal skills.

"It's important to know all about tactics and techniques," said Ben Jernigan, a highly successful franchise salesman, "but it's equally important to know how to *look, feel,* and *talk* like a power negotiator."

Jernigan, who admits to finding himself in the underdog role in negotiations because he is "basically an introvert," has found ingenious ways of gaining the upper hand against more powerful negotiators. These important techniques are discussed in Chapter 11.

Negotiating a Raise or Better Job

If you're seeking a better job, or higher pay (and who isn't?) this chapter is definitely for you:

G. M. Dozier, a senior officer of a major executive search firm, reveals little-known secrets about landing top jobs, either on your own or through a competent third party.

Separate chapters are devoted to those perennial negotiators—buyers and sellers.

As a seller, you'll find out how to understand buyers' needs, counter buyers' favorite tactics, and use effective questioning techniques to get your way.

As a buyer, you'll learn how to counter sellers' tactics, deal with "last and final offers," negate phony offers, and exchange small favors for big ones.

Dealing in Business and Industry

Chapter 15 deals with power negotiation in business and industry—both from the superior's and the subordinate's point of view.

Finally, you'll learn how to stage and conduct a formal negotiation; how to pick your team; how to set an agenda in your favor; how to establish ground rules; and how to gain power leverage by using a devil's advocate rehearsal technique.

David V. Lewis

CONTENTS

15

Chapter 1

HOW THE PROS USE POWER IN NEGOTIATING

Ben Thompson is adept at influencing the way others *feel* and *think*. As a result he usually "gets his way" in his dealing with others. This makes him, for practical purposes, a power negotiator.

Power negotiators are usually made, not born. And when you observe Ben in action—first with his wife, then a client, and finally his boss—you'll begin to get some idea of what makes a power negotiator tick.

ON BUYING A HOME

Ben and his wife Martha had outgrown their home, so they decided to move to a larger one; however, they disagreed sharply on *where* to buy. Martha, somewhat of a social climber, had her eyes set on a two-story house in an older but highly prestigious section of town. Ben, a fisherman and boat enthusiast, was equally adamant about buying a lake-front home. In fact, he had already spotted an excellent buy—a lake home that had been on the market for several months.

Sensing a deadlock with Martha on the issue, Ben launched his well-thought-out negotiation strategy. First, he "permitted" Martha to buy a limited edition painting she had coveted for some time. Shortly thereafter, he *encouraged* her to buy an antique clock that he had always considered too expensive. And finally, he agreed to her long-term desire to completely refurnish their home in Early American.

Ben Makes (and Takes) Concessions

Ben obviously made several concessions. Significantly, they were all rather expensive furnishings for their home. But *which* home? The one at the lake, of course!

Ben successfully used one of the oldest, but still one of the most effective, negotiation techniques around. He swapped several minor concessions for what to him was a major one—that new home on the lake where he would spend many "profitable" hours for the rest of his life.

As we'll discuss more fully later, there's an art to making concessions. Power negotiators like Ben realize that even less experienced negotiators are usually willing to swap several small concessions for one big one.

Negotiating the Price Down

Ben exhibited his negotiating prowess even further in buying the lake home. The property was listed originally for $135,000. After two months, the builder dropped the sales price to $125,000, which he declared to be "rock bottom."

However, after two more months passed without the home selling, Ben assumed rather confidently that the builder would drop his price still further. The assumption was based on more than a mere hunch. Through a mutual friend, Ben found out the builder had been paying a very high interim interest rate for nearly a year.

As a result, Ben made a firm take-it-or-leave-it offer of $115,000. The builder rejected the offer outright at first, but called back the next day. "It's a deal," he said.

Ben's strategy worked for several reasons, but mainly because of his ability to make solid assumptions—another characteristic of the power negotiator.

Ben Deals with a Client

Then there's that transaction with a client. Shortly after joining a Houston management consulting firm, Ben landed a lucrative contract for his company with a Fortune 500 manufacturer. What made the sale a genuine coup was the fact that every other major consulting firm in the area had tried unsuccessfully for over a year to get the business.

Was it beginner's luck for Ben? Apparently not. He successfully negotiated the contract on his first call, mainly because he was able to zero in on his client's problem almost instantly—a feat others apparently hadn't been able to do.

Pinpointing the Real Problem

Before calling on the prospect, Ben found out everything he could about the company's operation and its top management people. He did so by researching the library's business section and interviewing a number of employees.

The problem, Ben discovered, was a high turnover rate in middle and upper management ranks. The turnover appeared to be caused mainly by poor communication. Problems either weren't reaching top management, or they were so watered down by the time they got there that the *real* problem never came into focus.

As a result, top management was not being responsive to managers' real needs. Thus the heavy quit rate and resultant confusion in management ranks.

Ben discovered further that the owner and founder, D. Blair Dalton, kept too tight a rein on his chief administrators. He simply had not learned to delegate successfully, and this created further discontent.

Satisfying Their Needs

Ben confronted Dalton with the problem head on, explaining that the *need to know and understand* was a vital basic need that was being denied under the present organizational setup. He then outlined a detailed plan—one that had proved successful in other industrial situations—as a solution to the problem. His presentation, supplemented by testimonials from other big firms that had had the same problem, was convincing—so much so that Dalton signed a contract on the spot.

Ben thus exhibited two other characteristics of a power negotiator: thorough research and accommodation of the needs of others. In this case, two basic needs—self-esteem, and knowledge and understanding—were not being met adequately in the organization. We'll discuss these needs more fully in the next chapter.

Ben Seeks Recognition Himself

Not long after landing the manufacturing contract, Ben decided it was time to make a bid for a move up in his company, a big move! He requested not merely a raise, but part of the action—a partnership in the company.

Here was a situation that would test Ben's negotiating mettle. He would be dealing with someone who had superior power, and in all likelihood, at least equal negotiating powers.

COPING WITH POWER

How did Ben negotiate such a deal? He understood the nature of power and exploiting one of its basic principles: Knowledge and expertise can be great sources of power.

Ben made a strong case by showing, in dollars and cents, how his landing the manufacturing account had improved the company's financial position. He also exhibited in the interview a grasp of the entire organization, even suggesting ways in which the organization might profitably expand.

Thus Ben showed another of the requisites of a power negotiator: The ability to hold his own, even when negotiating as the underdog, which we all are at one time or another.

HOW A POWER NEGOTIATOR DOES IT

Ben ranks as a power negotiator because he has

- A deep understanding of the nature of power.

- A high self-image, and thus equally lofty expectation level.

- An ability to size up people and situations and to make valid assumptions about both.

- The common sense to let the other person get *something* from the negotiation.

The idea is to relate these principles to situations you run into in your daily business and social activities. With practice, you can improve your negotiating ability dramatically. For starters, let's take a look at the basic principles of power.

USING THE PRINCIPLES OF POWER

You can sometimes have power even if you have little or no power.

A teen-ager, for example, is normally "powerless" in negotiating with his parents. But it doesn't always have to work that way.

James, for example, is a 17-year-old senior-high student who is having trouble at school.

"Shape up," the father warns, "or I'll cut off your allowance and ground you."

"That's fine with me" the youngster says. "I'm tired of school anyway. I'll get a job next week and move into an apartment."

"But what about college—and that law degree?" the father complains.

"What about it?" the teen-ager replies belligerently.

Who eventually "won" this negotiation? At least for the moment, the powerless teen-ager.

Jim Walton Gets His Way

Take the case of Jim Walton, Chief of Public Relations for a conglomerate. He is trying to negotiate a bigger budget for his understaffed department.

"Money's too tight right now," the boss says. "Talk to me next year."

"All right," the chief responds, "but we'll have to cut back on some of our projects we'd planned, including the profiles on you and other top executives. Too bad, I think the Sunday supplements would have bought the idea. I think it would have helped your image, too." Three days later, the chief got his increased budget okayed.

Bill Blackmon Finds Key to Success

Salespeople almost always find themselves in an "underdog" position. After all, most buyers can shop around for the best deal.

However, top salespeople like Bill Blackmon of Fort Worth fail to concede this point automatically. "It's bad business to *always* assume that the buyer is in the driver's seat," Blackmon said. "Sometimes, it's the other way around; the salesperson has an edge."

Blackmon, who sells sophisticated electronic components, cites one such instance when he was dealing with a major aerospace firm.

"Several top firms would be bidding for the business," he said, "so my first inclination was to come in with a pretty low bid.

"However, I made a couple of important discoveries in doing my homework. First, I found out that the aerospace firm would require an unusually large volume of components and at a very early date. Meeting schedule was critical for them. In surveying the list of potential bidders, I judged that we were one of only two companies capable of meeting these demands.

"Then I found out through my 'spy network' in the aerospace firm that the Vice President of Engineering had a strong preference for my company's product."

Armed with these valuable inputs, Blackmon entered the negotiation with a reasonably high expectation level. He demanded—and got—a relatively high price for his product.

Next time you enter a negotiation as the underdog, take a hard look at the other party's position. He or she might be more vulnerable than you think. This approach requires an inquisitive mind and a creative approach to negotiation, coupled with total dedication to the task at hand.

POWER MUST BE ACKNOWLEDGED

Power exists to the degree it is accepted. This third principle is frequently used as a *defensive* strategy. It consists, in the main, of finding ways to neutralize the power status of the opposition.

Alfred Adler's contention that we constantly strive to raise ourselves from inferiority to superiority, from a non-power to a power position, seems to hold water. And though competition tends to create quality in business, too much of it can cause problems in negotiating. This is an issue we'll explore in the next chapter.

To be sure, competition characterizes most negotiations. In almost any transaction, one person *assumes* a more powerful position—real or imagined—by dint of superior knowledge, appearance, age, education, or what have you.

The person with power naturally tends to fare better in negotiations. Research, for example, shows that people who are middle-aged, college-educated, well-dressed and good-looking can practically write their own ticket in the negotiating game. Check this out in your daily activities and see if it is not so.

How Underdogs Gain Advantage

If this is true, again how can the underdog in the
negotiation—the person with less power—gain parity? In
many cases, by refusing to "accept" the other person's more
powerful position, or by finding ingenious ways to *minimize* it.

The latter course is usually preferable, since circumstances frequently dictate just how far you can go in
avoiding another's power position. For example, a corporal
can't normally practice one-upmanship on his commanding
officer, and the boss-subordinate relationship in industry
usually calls for a relatively high degree of conformity.

But it *can* be done! Especially if you as underdog are
diplomatic and subtle in your approach. The idea is not to
blatantly ignore the other person's power position, but to find
ways to work around it.

For example, listen in on this brief conversation between
a young internal auditor from corporate headquarters (little
power) talking with the vice president of a division (high
power).

Auditor "Challenges" Superior

Manager: We'll cooperate 100 percent. But we need this
audit done in a hurry. My staff's snowed under with other
projects right now.

Auditor: How fast?

Manager: Two days . . . at the outside!

Auditor: I'm not sure we can complete the job that fast.

Manager: Why not?

Auditor: Well, we have orders from Corporate to take a
detailed look at all political donations and expense accounts.
It's all because of the mess at the Houston Division last year.
Remember?

Manager: I sure do. What a kick that was! Well, if that's what Corporate wants . . . how long would you estimate all this will take?

Auditor: At least a week, working overtime.

Manager: Well, do the best you can. And incidentally, better check with me when you audit expense reports. There are a few things I might need to explain.

Neutralizing Authority

The auditor didn't ignore nor defy the vice president; he simply found a very clever way to work around the request. In effect, he somewhat neutralized the Vice President's power position with a ploy of his own. The ploy can be real or imagined, depending on whom you're dealing with and the stakes involved.

Power negotiators use these three basic principles skillfully in their daily transactions. In addition, they are acutely aware of power sources, which they learn to draw on continually—and expertly. The most commonly used power sources are listed on the following pages.

KNOWLEDGE IS PRIME POWER SOURCE

Knowledge. Almost everyone knows "knowledge is power"; power negotiators seem to be the only ones who consistently do something about it.

People in "knowledge professions"—doctors, lawyers, engineers, scientists, top executives and the like—generally negotiate from a position of power simply because of their known expertise.

But this doesn't mean you have to rule yourself out as a power negotiator, simply because you don't have a Ph.D. You can often gain roughly the same power status by acquiring a special body of knowledge in almost any area—by becoming, in effect, an expert.

Larry Wilson Gains Leverage

Larry Wilson, for example, started as an associate in the accounting department of a big Houston energy company. He soon discovered that he had little leverage with his peers, since he didn't have an accounting degree, and even less clout in negotiating with his boss.

Being somewhat of a power negotiator by inclination, Larry started looking for ways to raise his power base. This was in the time frame when computers were being introduced into some of the bigger companies.

He read books, attended seminars and talked to experts on the subject. In fairly short order, he was highly conversant in computer knowledge and know-how.

Larry's effort paid off. Shortly thereafter, the company *did* get heavily involved in computers. Larry cheerfully lent his expertise. In short order, he was able to negotiate not only a substantial raise, but a promotion to boot.

Knowing that knowledge is power is not enough. You'll need to do something about it if you're to become a true power negotiator.

APPEARANCE MAKES BIG DIFFERENCE

Appearance. Phillip T. Molloy, whom *Time Magazine* tagged as America's first "wardrobe engineer," claims that men and women who dress for success get preferential treatment in the business world. They also tend to get an upper hand in most of their negotiations.

Thus coming to the negotiating table well dressed and well groomed can often give you the slight edge you need to negotiate successfully. This is especially true, researchers have found, of well-dressed men negotiating with women.

How a Realtor Was an Exception

There are, of course, exceptions to every rule. For instance, a wealthy Texas Realtor got his start by buying and renting a lot of shacks in a downtrodden part of town. He would personally show up every Saturday morning to collect rent. Though becoming richer every year, he dressed rather shabbily when he made his rounds, figuring that poor people didn't much cotton to paying rent to a rich landlord decked out in a Brooks Brothers suit.

The dress habit became so ingrained in the Realtor's thinking that he continued to dress sloppily, even after he made it very big financially, but by that time it really didn't matter. His *known* power source was now his money.

STATUS IS SIGNIFICANT SOURCE

Position. The head of an insurance company sent one of his young new adjusters to settle a sizable fire-damage claim from one of his oldest and most prestigious clients.

The client rejected the company's offer, which by all standards was a fair one. Realizing this, the insurance company president called his client to see what went wrong.

"The offer wasn't all that bad," the client said, "but that young adjuster of yours just didn't seem to want to consider any alternatives. Besides, it seems as much business as we've done with you, you'd have sent one of your senior men to handle this case—a vice president at least."

Gets Title and Raise

Next week, the young adjuster was given a more imposing title (and a modest raise) in order to hide his "junior status." Something worked, for the company never got another complaint about the young adjuster.

Titles do carry weight, and it remains a deep mystery to me why more companies don't recognize this and give their people more authoritative ones. It doesn't cost much more, if anything, and it *can* add to their negotiating power, especially when negotiating with people outside their own organizations.

USING INFORMATION TO GAIN ADVANTAGE

Information. As opposed to knowledge, information implies data gathering for a specific purpose rather than assembling a body of knowledge, usually over a longer period of time.

For example, Dick James, a commercial real estate broker, was attempting to sell a tract of land between Fort Worth and Dallas, some time before the area burgeoned into one of the fastest growing areas in the country.

Negotiations were long and hard, and after a week, the two principals were still more than a million dollars apart.

Dick then started an intensive search for data which might give him leverage. He got voluminous reports from the Chamber of Commerce, a detailed prospectus on the proposed mammoth Dallas-Fort Worth International Airport, and other "confidential" reports.

Armed with this information, Dick put together an attractive color-slide show. The client was so impressed that he bought the property immediately, at very close to the list price.

"LEGITIMACY" AS POWER SOURCE

Legitimacy. A national real estate franchise issues a "certificate" to home owners who list their property with one of its offices. It is a warranty, printed in fancy script type on parchment paper, and it guarantees the seller prompt action if he's not satisfied with the service he's getting.

Though very "official looking," the piece of paper is just that. It offers the home owner little more than the broker's *word* that he will make prompt amends if things don't work out as promised. It is *not* legally binding. But people accept it as such because it has the *look* and *feel* of *legitimacy*.

There is a strong tendency to take "official" documents and symbols, such as contracts, diplomas, class rings, lapel pins, and the like, at face value. They can sometimes add to your power base in negotiation.

Politicians, entertainers, sports stars and others of this ilk sometimes use high-powered press agents to build their public image. It gives these people great negotiating leverage when it comes to negotiating for ballots or bucks.

MAKING MONEY AND POLITICS PAY OFF

Money and politics. Whoever said "money is power" knew whereof he spoke—and when money talks, almost everyone listens.

The advantage of having money, from the negotiation point of view, is that it gives you credibility in other areas. The word of a "rich person" carries more weight on just about any subject than it normally deserves.

Being able to manipulate issues and people politically is another prime source of power. The late Lyndon B. Johnson is an example of the power of political negotiating.

Politics is not confined to the White House. It permeates the business world and can become a source of power in just about any organization.

There are other sources of power, but these are probably the prime ones in negotiation. You'll need to cultivate as many of these sources as possible in order to enhance your position as a power negotiator.

HOW TO MAKE ASSUMPTIONS

You should, by all means, make well-conceived assumptions about what position your opponent is *likely* to take. You should also try to figure out in advance how he or she will probably react to *your* strategy. In fact, making valid assumptions should be the end result of a thorough planning session. Good planning, in effective negotiation as in good management, is the key to success.

On the other hand, you shouldn't make emotional or too hastily conceived assumptions. For as you'll be admonished in virtually every beginning business training session you attend: When you assume, you make an *ass* of *u* and *me*. Trite, but still true!

So the answer is a resounding yes; in most cases you'll definitely need to make assumptions about your opposition. But making assumptions is only half the story. The other half lies in testing to see if they are valid. This separates the so-so negotiator from the power negotiator.

Negotiating for a Home

For example, let's *assume* you're in the market for a larger home. You respond to a newspaper ad by an owner, which says, in effect, "For sale by owner. Immaculate 4-bedroom, 3-bath home on beautiful wooded lot."

In your call, you discover that the owner is a middle-aged woman, recently widowed, living with her mother. The home has 3,000 square feet, and the asking price is $90,000.

Having these and a few other facts, you make the following basic assumptions: The widow is anxious to sell (the urgency in her voice told you so), and she will likely come down in price, perhaps by as much as $5,000; she is *not* knowledgeable in real estate and will not drive a hard bargain; she will probably be willing to take a contingency contract, enabling you to sell your home before buying hers. Another assumption is that the widow is asking more for the property than it's worth.

Setting "Low" and "High" Limits

Based on these assumptions, you mentally set your minimum price at $80,000 and your top price at $85,000.

Then comes the actual negotiation. After exchanging amenities, you inspect the home, paying special attention to needed repairs in an effort to justify your low offer.

To test your assumption that the seller is probably not

knowledgeable in real estate, you mention that *if* you were to buy, you would probably get a GI loan. The widow responds that she doesn't want to sell under a VA loan because she would have to pay discount points.

Your assumption is obviously wrong. Based on this and other responses, you realize that the widow obviously knows a thing or two about real estate. Thus mentally, you *concede* that you would have to get a conventional loan at a slightly higher interest rate.

Price Assumption Is Correct

You find that another assumption—that she is anxious to sell—is correct. She has already selected a lot and started construction on a condominium at the lake. She should be willing to make at least a minor price concession in order to get a good contract.

The bottom line on the negotiation was this. After rejecting your $80,000 offer on a contingency contract, the widow offered to drop her price to $87,500.

You counter with a final $85,000 offer on a conventional contract (which would reduce seller expense), and she accepts.

Thus some of your assumptions prove valid: others don't. Like most successful power negotiators, you are flexible enough to swap concessions. But in the end, you didn't do badly: $5,000 off a solid list price.

A negotiation is not unlike a boxing match between two pros. These experienced boxers will normally spend a round or two feeling each other out—looking for openings and figuring out the opponent's "game plan."

Studies Condone "Sparring"

In over 200 studies, social psychologists found that negotiations are usually more "successful" when opposing parties spend about 30 minutes or so at the outset of negotiations getting to know each other. This time, they contend, should be spent in stressing similarities and establishing expertness on the issues involved. Less "sparring" time would naturally be spent on shorter negotiations.

Perhaps the chief value of making assumptions is that it enables you to play your own devil's advocate. You can constantly ask—and answer—questions like: What will I say or do if my opponent says this . . . or that? It is one of the most effective ways to arrive at logical assumptions and build tenable positions.

ROLES OF CONCESSIONS AND EXPECTATION LEVEL

Negotiations almost always involve making *concessions*. Regardless of how proficient you become at power negotiating, there'll be times when you have to "give" as much as you "take."

But power negotiators know not only *how* and *when* to make concessions, but *why*. Studies on the subject show clearly that negotiators with higher *expectation levels* usually win out over those who do not routinely *expect* to fare so well in the transaction. Negotiators who have a high expectation level and who are skilled at negotiating almost always win.

Expectation Level Fluctuates

One's expectation level is rarely constant. It usually goes up and down several times in any lengthy negotiation.

For example, in negotiating for the widow's home, the buyer entered the negotiation with a relatively high expectation level. He had done his homework, and made what appeared to be some valid assumptions. Still, his expectation level probably ran the gamut during the transaction.

It dropped perceptibly when the widow showed a stronger-than-expected knowledge of real estate, and again when she refused to accept a contingency contract. But it rebounded when she finally agreed to drop her price to $85,000.

What Affects Expectation Level?

What causes a negotiator's expectation level to remain consistently high? There are many factors, no doubt, not the least of which is knowledge of the issues at hand and the ability to make sound assumptions. Beyond these factors, there is the critical element of self-image—the way you feel about yourself. High expectation level is almost always consistent with high self-image.

One way to enhance your *negotiating* self-image is to become expert in negotiating techniques—the ones we'll explore in this book. Another is to consistently become steeped in the issues involved in the negotiation at hand.

The psychological factors of self-image are beyond the purview of this book. Briefly, however, they entail reviewing your past performance, your attitudes and other intangible factors to determine the probable cause of your self-image being what it is.

For now, it's sufficient to recognize that power negotiation entails a high expectation level, which has a direct bearing on the concessions you will make—or fail to make—in your negotiations.

AVOIDING THE FIRST OFFER

Generally, you will want to avoid accepting the first offer in almost any negotiation. In most cases, you have little to lose by holding out for a higher offer. More likely than not, it is expected.

For example, on a recent trip to Acapulco—my first visit to Mexico—I went shopping for a few gifts. I was accompanied by a cab driver, who also served as my "guide."

When he discovered that I paid the full price for every item, he almost gagged. "Never accept the first offer," he said. "In Mexico, they *expect* you to bargain." He was right. Some of the gifts I bought after that were purchased by as much as half the asking price.

HOW TO SWAP CONCESSIONS

Another guideline followed by most power negotiators is to swap several minor concessions for a major one.

For example, a friend of mine felt he was at long last gaining the "upper hand" in his marriage. During a short period of time, his wife had agreed to let him play golf twice a week; agreed to his adding a couple of suits to his wardrobe; and agreed to let him take a weekend fishing trip with the boys.

Now it was the wife's turn to ask for a concession, and it was a big one: an $8,500 sports car. Arithmetically, it turned out to be a pretty good deal for the power-negotiating spouse.

Concession making is an art. When possible, make minor concessions in return for larger ones. On the defensive side, you don't necessarily have to swap concessions at all if your position is strong enough. Simply let the other party make them.

POWER NEGOTIATING IN A NUTSHELL

In summary, the key points in becoming a power negotiator are:

- Master and use the basic principles of power.
- Identify and frequently use the primary sources of power.
- Make assumptions as part of your planning.
- Develop a consistently strong expectation level, based on a strong self-image.
- Learn the fine art of making concessions.

Chapter 2

MAKING NEGOTIATION A WIN-WIN PROPOSITION

Bob Woodruff is purchasing agent for a southern-based manufacturer of fertilizer materials. For years, he has purchased potash, an ingredient used in fertilizer, from Henry Moore, a local distributor.

The arrangement has worked quite well. Henry's prices are competitive, and he has bent over backward to make sure orders are delivered on schedule, an important factor for Bob.

Recently, however, the supply of potash increased significantly, forcing the price down. Instead of negotiating a price adjustment with Henry, Bob decided to open his business up to all bidders.

Bob Returns Bids

Bob was swamped with bids, including several which were obviously trying to "buy in." The overwhelming response told Bob that he was now clearly in the driver's seat. As a result, he sent all bids back with a note saying, in effect, "You are going to have to do better than this."

This tactic, which is discussed more fully in a later chapter, *appears* to be a bona fide power negotiating maneuver.

And it *did* work. An out-of-state bidder reduced its price drastically and won Bob's business. Henry was left holding the bag.

Bob won the "battle," but lost the "war." When potash was again in short supply, he could get none and his production was delayed. This is frequently the fate of negotiators who exploit rather than bargain in good faith; who deceive rather than deal in a straightforward fashion; who regard power negotiation as strictly a win-lose, rather than a win-win, proposition.

HOW TO WIN "GRACEFULLY"

This is not to say that you shouldn't negotiate to win—and win decisively! Nor does it preclude your being aggressive and resourceful, using all the "tricks" at your disposal. But the truly effective power negotiator goes a step further; he negotiates with an eye to letting the other party get *something* out of the transaction, if nothing more than minor concessions, or at a minimum, his self-esteem. This is really what power negotiating is all about.

It is little wonder, then, that most of us, like Bob Woodruff, are given to win-lose negotiating. We're programmed to do so. In sports, we're led to believe that winning is everything. The adversary position in law leads to win-lose situations. Negotiating between management and labor is routinely marked by confrontation and ultimatum. Unfortunately, many business negotiations take on the aura of a gunfight at high noon; somebody has got to be done in!

Cooperative Attitude Sought

Most studies show that an overly competitive nature can lead to many problems in negotiating. Researchers claim that "competitors" are often insensitive to others' needs in negotiation. Further, competitive types tend to be less likely to vary their behavior pattern, causing many of their negotiations to end in deadlock.

On the other hand, negotiators who take a basically cooperative position appear to be more sensitive to others' needs and adjust more easily to others' negotiating style and strategy. They are capable of using a gentle touch, but they can put on "brass knucks" if necessary to counter a strong competitive negotiator. Ideally, the power negotiator should fit this cooperative mold.

Why Cooperation Helps

When you stop and think about it, the rationale behind win-win negotiating is solid. Both parties enter the negotiation *thinking* there is something in it for them. They may clearly see their opponent has an edge; nonetheless, they expect to gain something from the transaction. Otherwise, why bother to negotiate at all?

It is when we gain absolutely nothing from a negotiation that we feel defeated and frustrated. Under these circumstances, we frequently vow to "get even." And if humiliated deeply enough, we *do* eventually find some way to even the score. This is why the skilled mediator can be such a valuable addition to a negotiation. As an objective third party, he can provide both parties with a "graceful retreat." He can, in other words, convert a deadlock into a win-win proposition.

Most Negotiations Aren't "Final"

There are several reasons why you can profit from a win-win philosophy in negotiation. Foremost, perhaps, is the fact that many of your business negotiations are *not* final. You are likely to have further business transactions with the other party somewhere along the line. If you have been *fair* in your previous negotiations, regardless of how hard a bargain you might have driven, your future negotiations with that party are almost certain to be more harmonious and productive. If not, your opponent will probably be vindictive.

In the chapters that follow, we'll reveal a variety of power tactics and techniques. If you'll master these techniques, using a strong cooperative posture, you can be well on your way to becoming a power negotiator par excellence.

INNOVATIVE ATTITUDE NEEDED

In order to become an effective win-win negotiator, you'll need to find some ingenious ways to let the other party salvage something from negotiations. That something is most likely to be in the form of basic human needs.

Behavioral psychologists tell us we're a bundle of human needs. When our needs are substantially met, we generally feel good about things; when they're not met, we feel threatened and dissatisfied.

Basically, these needs include those for:

Well-being. Including the most basic need for food, water and sex, and the slightly higher need for safety and security.

Self-esteem. Ego might well be the biggest little word in the dictionary. The Chinese came up with the idea several centuries ago and called it "saving face." It is beyond doubt one of the most important of human needs.

Achievement. Abraham Maslow calls this need *self-actualization*, the need to live up to the best within yourself. Since you obviously won't be "achieving" a great deal when you come out second best in a negotiation, you'll have to be especially ingenious to find ways to satisfy your opponent's achievement needs when he comes out second best.

Knowledge and understanding. Why has America spent vast sums to put a man on the moon and probe deep into space? Because of an insatiable curiosity about our universe that must be satisfied. Almost everyone is deeply curious about what's going on around him. When uninformed, people often feel threatened. This is an excellent point to remember in negotiation.

Let's discuss these needs briefly as they relate to power

negotiating. Bear in mind, it's not an easy thing to win in negotiation and at the same time accommodate others' needs. But then, no one said becoming a power negotiator was an easy thing.

HOW TO SATISFY WELL-BEING NEEDS

If you were lost in the desert, you would no doubt exchange your worldly possessions for a small canteen of water. And if I were to force you to do so, I would be a most opportunistic win-lose negotiator. After you survived your ordeal, my guess is that you would be highly vindictive if the shoe were on the other foot in a future negotiation. And I would speculate further that you would go out of your way to see that such a negotiation took place.

How could I have negotiated the canteen of water in a win-win way, enabling you to gain something from the negotiation? One way would have been to take only *part* of your fortune in exchange for the water (depending on how wealthy you were) or, even if I took a larger sum, I might have helped you to "get on your feet" later, as the Allies did after defeating Germany and Japan after World War II.

Safety, Security Needs Stressed

It is the upper levels of the need for well-being—the needs for safety and security—that become paramount in the economic world in which most of us operate.

In the boss-subordinate relationship, for example, the boss is, in a sense, always "negotiating" for higher performance from his employees. He can *demand* a certain minimum level of performance, but how does he negotiate that extra effort? If he's smart, he appeals to the employee's basic needs.

Sid Wilkes Changes Style

For example, Sid Wilkes, production manager for an Oklahoma manufacturing firm, had a reputation as a demanding, authoritative boss. "Get that production out—or else!" was his philosophy, and he got this point across to his foremen almost daily.

Sid got his department's production up, all right, but in the process, he developed an unacceptable employee turn-over rate, especially among his foremen. This ultimately led to *lower* production, not to mention pressing personnel and morale problems.

When Personnel started conducting exit interviews, they discovered foremen under Sid were either leaving the company to find a more secure position, or going back to a job on the line, where union membership afforded them more security.

Sid discovered (the hard way) that many people do not function well under constant threat to their security. He gradually learned to "negotiate" with each foreman on an individual basis. He was no less demanding, and he kept the same high production standards. He simply found new ways to negotiate with his employees.

He motivated them through raises and promotion, of course. But more important, he was able to create a sense of security and well being, when appropriate, through more effective interpersonal relations. As a result, his production increased and his personnel problems were greatly reduced.

Service Station Operator "Succeeds"

The gasoline shortage of the late 1970's posed a threat to the well-being of many. Most people have to drive to get to work. Thus many felt threatened when gas stations started closing down early, and limiting supplies when they were open.

Service station operators, who up to this point had found themselves relatively low on the socioeconomic pole, suddenly were able to write their own ticket. They could negotiate any price they wanted, to *whom* they cared to do business with.

Some operators, realizing the shortage would end some-day, became what I consider to be expert negotiators. They satisfied customer security needs in several ways. Perhaps the most ingenious way was to sell gas to *regular* customers first (at high but not exorbitant prices), and to "outsiders" as supply lasted.

So even though customers "lost" on the gas price negotiation, they gained a sense of well-being as a result of the operator's thoughtful policy.

THE IMPORTANCE OF SELF-ESTEEM

Everyone likes to feel important. If you have doubts, send telegrams to about a dozen or so of your friends, saying simply, "Congratulations!" I'd be greatly surprised if most of the recipients wouldn't say, "It's about time someone recognized what I'm doing."

Recognizing an opponent's strong points, or in many instances letting him "save face," is one of the stronger points you can concede to a "losing opponent."

For example, early during my checkered career, I spent a comparatively short stint as a labor relations analyst. Our chief was Ted Young, a rugged individualist who it seemed to me asked no quarter—and certainly gave none—at the negotiating table. Union officials considered him a double-tough adversary.

Ted Has Upper Hand

I first saw Ted negotiate with the union during a year when the company was laying off in droves because of government cutbacks in spending. This put the company, represented by Ted, in an excellent position to turn down union demands, which they did.

In fact, things went so badly for the union during the negotiation that I began to actually feel sorry for the union negotiators. So tough was Ted in his demands that I feared union officials would surely lose their jobs.

But near the end of negotiations, Ted did two things

which curbed my fears, and I'm sure, those of the union negotiators.

Ted had reduced the union's heavy pay-increase demands dramatically. He also managed to "win" on most big issues, such as seniority rights, fringe benefits and the like.

Ted Concedes Minor Points

Then, in somewhat of a turnabout, he seemed to "allow" the union to win on a number of relatively minor issues, such as adding dental benefits and an additional holiday.

Ted's final gesture was even more revealing. In front of top union officials, Ted lauded his opponent as one of the shrewdest, fairest and ablest negotiators in the business.

The union official undoubtedly "lost" the proceedings to a well-prepared power negotiator. Yet he was able to win minor concessions and, perhaps even more important, keep his all-important self-esteem and status as a professional negotiator relatively intact.

Tables Are Turned

He also kept his professional relationship with Ted on an even keel, a fact which served Ted in good stead at similar negotiations three years later. This time, the tables had turned. The company had big new contracts and tight development schedules. It simply could not afford labor problems. So this time, the company had to accede to many union demands. But the union negotiator, remembering Ted's track record for fairness and recognizing the need to maintain a cooperative atmosphere, allowed Ted to gain minor concessions—and to *sustain* his reputation.

A hint to the wise should be sufficient. But it took at least one more incident to convince me that satisfying others' needs through win-win negotiation is usually the best route to take.

Home Seller Negotiates Price

This time I was trying to list an owner's property for my real estate firm. Shortly into the interview, I asked the owner point blank what price he wanted. "I want $75,000 and not a penny less!" he said. At the same time, he glanced at his wife as if to say, "See, that's how you negotiate with these real estate people." Unfortunately, I was soon to discover that my interpretation of this non-verbal message was indeed accurate.

Actually my market analysis showed the property to be worth $69,000—tops! I labored long and hard to show the seller the pitfalls of listing too high, but to no avail. He had *committed* himself to the $75,000 price *before his wife*, and that was that.

Looking back, I was much too rigid in my position, too. The inevitable result was a deadlock, which meant that I didn't get the listing.

Lesson Is Learned

Looking back again, I think the only way to have won that negotiation would have been to list the property at $75,000. He would no doubt have come down in price a little later. But to have admitted that he was wrong in front of his wife would have been too damaging to his ego.

After that, I rarely asked a seller up front what he wanted for his property. Instead, I justified my listing price with recent comparable neighborhood sales and negotiated from a position of relative strength. This approach precluded his having to "back down" from a too high initial asking price.

It was at this point that I became intensely interested in the subject of power negotiating. If it worked in the limited areas in which I had seen it in action, would it work elsewhere? Based on years of observation of power negotiating in action, and on my own experiences, the answer has to be a resounding "Yes!" Power negotiating is a philosophy that will work efficiently in almost any situation, whether it be between friends, companies or nations.

Third Parties Affect Ego Needs

But back for a moment to this matter of ego needs. It is never more evident than when third parties are present in a negotiation. Researchers point out this classic example:

A married couple had been shopping for a new car. They finally found one they really wanted, listed at $6,900. "Let me handle this," the husband told his wife. "I'll offer $5,000 at first, and eventually go as high as $5,500 if I have to. That's how you deal for a new car." The wife saw nothing wrong with the original low offer of $5,000. But since she wanted the car very badly, she insisted he be more flexible on his final price. "Nothing doing," he said. "Let *me* show you how to save money."

The husband made the $5,000 first offer and predictably, the salesman said his company would lose money at that price. "Do you want us to lose on a deal?" he asked.

After reaching what appeared to be a deadlock in negotiating the price, the salesman brought his sales manager into the act. He told him his plan was to try hard for $6,000 but finally settle for $5,500 if he had to.

Ego Kills a Deal

With the wife and sales manager now sitting in as "spectators," the negotiation took a strange turn. Despite the fact that both parties had *mentally* agreed to a $5,500 final price, neither would make the final price concession.

Why the impasse? Because both the husband and the salesman had committed themselves in front of third parties to a rigid price position. To have "backed down" would have resulted in a severe jolt to self-esteem. *Egos* obviously stood in the way of a final price that would have been acceptable to both parties.

Self-esteem can be *that* important in negotiating. Keep this in mind when you're negotiating at any level, especially if third parties are involved.

CASHING IN ON THE NEED TO KNOW AND UNDERSTAND

As previously mentioned, America is spending billions to explore outer space. Why? Because man has an insatiable need to *know and understand.* Fulfilling this basic need is still another way to let a "defeated" opponent salvage *something* from a negotiation.

For example, we have mentioned the importance of information as a source of power. Many executives realize this and are often reluctant to pass on bits of information which might give them a slight edge in the competitive executive suite. Such reluctance to give out information can pose a big problem in negotiating.

Why a Transfer Was Turned Down

For example, the manager of the marketing department in a big company badly wanted to transfer a talented young man who had gone to work recently in the firm's sales division. The marketing manager wanted the young man for a couple of reasons: he had writing ability, along with a knowledge of the food and beverage industry, in which the company was trying to make inroads.

Company protocol dictated that the marketing manager negotiate the transfer with the sales manager. At first, the sales manager declined. "Too valuable a man," he insisted. "We figure he'll be a section head in two years."

The marketing manager unsuccessfully appealed his case to higher authority. He then reopened his negotiation with the sales manager, only this time he told him the real reasons for wanting the young man in the marketing department.

"Why didn't you say so in the first place?" the Sales Manager said. "I think it'll be a big break for him."

Why the about face? Because the Sales Manager now *understood* the circumstances. Before, he secretly expected the marketing manager was trying to pull a "fast one" on him.

Using the Principle in Marriage

The need to know and understand is at the very heart of effective communication, which in turn is the basis of a sound marriage. And marriage, as one veteran counsellor put it, is "one negotiation after another."

For example, take the case of an executive we'll call Carl. Carl travels frequently and is away from home quite often. And even when he *is* home, Carl frequently works overtime, often spending the night in a Manhattan hotel rather than commuting late to his home in Connecticut.

Carl's wife, Patricia, became increasingly disenchanted with the setup, complaining frequently that she alone was raising the children and taking care of what little social life the couple had. Her complaining became so strong that it began to affect Carl's performance, both at home and at the office.

Carl Calls for Confrontation

Unable to resolve their problem in a day-to-day negotiation, Carl called for a "summit meeting." This time, he took a firm position. "Look," he said, "I work my tail off to support our comfortable life style. That's the way things have to be. Period."

Patricia complained but finally gave in to Carl's take-it-or-leave-it approach. Carl "won" the negotiation all right. But the "defeat" festered in Patricia's mind, and a month later, she filed for divorce.

Faced with the prospect of losing everything, Carl decided to renegotiate the problem. Only this time, he took a different tack.

Uses Different Approach

Carl came up with a detailed account of what it took to maintain the family lifestyle, including private school for the kids, a part-time maid, and a social life commensurate with his position. "The only way we can keep this up," he said, "is for me to continue at the current pace."

For the first time, perhaps, Patricia fully understood the situation, and understanding it, she accepted it, but not fully. Both sides made concessions. She agreed to cut back on some expenses; he agreed to spend more time at home, even if it affected his income somewhat.

Satisfying Achievement Needs

There must be a reason why executive placement agencies have grown so tremendously over the past two decades. A healthy economy has obviously created more executive openings. But I feel that perhaps the main reason for the heavy game of "executive musical chairs" is disenchantment with the organization. Many executives—at all levels—get the feeling they have reached a blind alley in their careers. They are not, as Maslow called it, self-actualizing—living up to their full potential.

Contrary to the Hollywood notion, there is definitely *not* room at the top. Only a comparative handful can reach the rarified atmosphere of the executive suite. The rest must either accept what they consider "mediocrity," or move on to greener pastures. Thus the proliferation of executive placement outfits.

How a Director Solved the Problem

The director of human resources of an oil company found himself in this dilemma. It was an older, established organization, with key men entrenched in most middle-management and upper-management jobs. This caused many promising young men to be either shoved into what they felt was a dead-end job, or simply ignored. As a result, promising young people were leaving the company at an abnormally high rate.

Negotiating with men and women over their professional careers is a demanding assignment at best. In this instance, the director of human resources was finding negotiations quite difficult because he could not, in good faith, promise too much.

Frustrated, the director called a consultant for help. The consultant suggested that in the absence of promotion, the director offer challenging assignments, which might give the bright young people a chance to use untapped capabilities.

New Assignments Help

The director of human resources followed this advice, when appropriate.

In one case, he put a promising young engineer who had been doing repetitive work on a job-rotation schedule. This opened up new challenges in marketing and administration. The new assignments enabled the engineer not only to use more of his talent, but made him feel he was "in the blueprint."

In still another instance, the director transferred a dissatisfied young personnel generalist to the company's west coast division. Though the job was similar, the change of scenery inspired the young lady to greater performance.

The problem of self-actualization in business and industry is a perennial one. Recognizing this, the director did what he could to solve this "negotiating problem."

Chapter 3

HOW TO USE
PACING AND TIMING
IN POWER NEGOTIATION

A number of years ago, I recall my city editor putting down a hard and fast deadline for the morning edition: all copy in by midnight except for late-breaking news stories of moment and late-ending ball games. No exceptions!

The same idea holds true for a newspaper or magazine ad. If you see a "hole" in either, it's probably because the ad agency didn't get the copy in on time.

To me these deadlines were *real*. For several reasons, notably fear I suppose, I almost always met them.

OTHER DEADLINES ARE IMAGINARY

On the other hand, there was that 6 p. m. dinner deadline I had as a youngster. I missed this one quite often, especially during the months when we could get in an extra inning or two of baseball before it turned dark.

Later, as a salesman, I remember showing a similar disdain for month-end reports. I didn't like to do them, and as long as I was meeting quota, I pretty well got them in when I felt like it.

These deadlines obviously didn't carry as much weight with me, so for practical purposes, they were *imaginary*.

The point of all this is that being able to use deadlines—real *or* imaginary—can enhance your position as a power negotiator.

How Jack Riddle Gained Leverage

For example, Jack Riddle, a real estate developer, used a deadline successfully in negotiating the purchase of a prime piece of property in the Houston area.

Almost any property in this burgeoning metropolis comes high. Naturally, this gives the property owner leverage in negotiating price.

At first, Riddle was considering one of two pieces of property owned by the seller, both roughly comparable in value. In an effort to "play down" the importance of the transaction, Riddle told the owner he was buying the land on speculation.

And he was—at first! But *during* the negotiation, Riddle got a commitment from an Eastern company that wanted to relocate its corporate headquarters in the Houston area.

A Switch in Strategy

Up to this point, Riddle had been negotiating heavily for Property A. He had come up on price—from an original $1.7 million offer to $2 million. On the other side, the owner originally asked for $2.8 million and was now quoting a "final price" of $2.5 million. They were a half million apart.

Suddenly, Riddle switched his attention to Property B, which had roughly the same acreage but was in a different part of town. "I'll give you $2.2 million for this property," he told the owner, "but I'm tired of haggling. I'll have to have your answer by noon tomorrow. Otherwise it's no deal. I've got another site in mind already."

Having issued his "final" offer, along with what appeared to be a legitimate deadline, Riddle waited anxiously in his office the next day to hear from the property owner. He had about given up, but at 10 minutes till 12:00, the phone rang. "I'll take $2.3 million," the owner said, "if you'll sign the deal over lunch."

"You're on," Riddle snapped back. "Bring the contract and I'll see you in 15 minutes at the Athletic Club."

Both Sides Benefit

In this case, the deadline worked as Riddle had hoped it would. He got a choice piece of property at a high, but not exorbitant price. He then signed a highly profitable deal with his Eastern client. The seller got a respectable price, including a face-saving concession from $2.2 to $2.3 million.

The deadline in this case was *imaginary*. Riddle could just as easily have signed the contract a week, or even a month hence. But the important point is, the seller *accepted the deadline as real*. It is indeed amazing how many times people will accept *your* deadline as *theirs*.

HOW YOU GAIN FROM USING DEADLINES

There are a number of advantages to be gained from using a deadline effectively.

In the first place, a deadline can create a sense of urgency. Negotiators tend to stall, hedge, and sometimes even lose interest if the transaction drags on too long. A deadline can sometimes bring things quickly into focus and cause one or both parties to *act*. Apparently, this is what happened in the above case.

Second, a deadline can prevent your opponent from gaining further knowledge and insight that might be used to give him leverage. In this case, for example, Riddle gave the seller only 24 hours in which to respond. Unless all the ground work had been done on the deal, including complex commercial appraisals and lengthy income projections, it would have been quite difficult for the seller to have come up with this valuable information in so short a time. Further, the deadline helped Riddle negotiate in comparative secrecy. Word of the deal would no doubt have surfaced soon. But not in 24 hours!

Finally, a deadline can give your opponent the *impression* that you're ready to deal. In this case, Riddle made his final offer with a "deal-or-get-off-the-pot" attitude that apparently convinced the seller he meant business. He *assumed* Riddle would back out if the deadline was not accepted.

Considering the Consequence

On the other hand, issuing a deadline carries a degree of risk, and in this case, a high one. What if the seller had been *intimidated* rather than "motivated" by Riddle's deadline? Riddle obviously would have been left holding the bag. The deadline technique, like other power negotiating tactics, must be used with skill and imagination.

This gets us back to one of the fundamentals of effective power negotiating—making valid assumptions about your opponent and the issues. Riddle "read" the seller correctly in this case and thus was able to use the deadline tactic successfully. Again, assumptions are based both on research during the planning stage of negotiation, and on observations made *during* the transaction.

Defending Against Deadlines

A successful power negotiator needs not only to master the tactics and techniques we'll mention in this book, but to find ways to successfully "defend" himself when such tactics are used by the opposition.

My advice is to take an in-depth look at the deadline. Why was it made? Is it real? What does the other party have to gain by setting it? What do you have to gain—or lose—by accepting it? And so forth.

As the recipient of the deadline, you'll have made some basic assumptions about the other party. Couple these assumptions with a hard-nosed analysis of the deadline and you'll likely know what course of action to take.

DEADLINES USED AT MANY LEVELS

Deadlines, properly executed, can be used effectively at just about any level of negotiation.

As a buyer, for example, you can insist on products being delivered within a certain time frame—or no deal! A housewife who was being given the runaround on the delivery of a new bedroom suite got prompt attention, but only after she told the store president, "Deliver it by Saturday morning or cancel the order." Most companies accept such deadlines as quite *real.*

Similarly, an organization can sometimes get negotiations off dead center by setting deadlines on mergers or acquisitions. Nations can often use the tactic successfully in negotiating a cease-fire or peace treaty.

How a Farmer Beat a Deadline

"Deadlines" of sorts are all around us, though most of them are not quite so dramatic as the ones just described. As a power negotiator, you'll need to know not only how to use deadlines effectively, but how to cope with them.

Merchants, for example, constantly remind us in full-page ads of impending deadlines: "Hurry! This spectacular sale *ends Saturday.*" Most such deadlines are real enough, all right. But not always. For instance, a farmer came to a major Dallas retail store one day after a huge appliance sale had ended. When informed that he was a day late, the farmer became angry and finally wanted to see the manager.

"Look," he said to the manager, "I drove 60 miles to buy your top-of-the-line refrigerator on sale. I don't care how your ad read in yesterday's paper. The only ad we saw was the ad you ran in our little weekly paper." After a bit more "negotiating," the farmer got his refrigerator at the sale price.

Why Not Test the Deadline?

This deadline was real enough, all right, to most of the buying public. But there are almost always exceptions. Stores are usually open approximately from 9 to 5, but under the right circumstances they might open early or stay late. Even the noted April 15 deadline for income tax can be extended in most cases. And if you fly the nation's airlines regularly, you will probably take their "deadlines" with a grain of salt.

Perhaps a good rule of thumb is: if you suspect that the deadline *might* not be ironclad, what have you got to lose by testing it?

Remember to use deadlines with care and prudence if you feel they will give you a negotiating edge. And don't fail to question deadlines imposed on you.

Parlaying Patience Into "Profit"

People tend to wait out deadlines until the last minute. Management-union negotiations are renowed for eleventh-hour settlements. The post office is all but swamped just before midnight of April 15—and the Houston property owner, you'll recall, waited until 10 minutes before the deadline expired before accepting Riddle's offer.

The point here is that *patience*—another proven negotiating tactic—is an integral part of using the deadline technique. Having the patience to "wait out" your opponent until the "last minute" can sometimes gain you valuable concessions in a negotiation.

There is much more, of course, to using *patience* as a primary weapon in negotiating. The United States learned this the hard way in Korea.

How Korea Used the Tactic

Here was America, the most powerful nation in the world, negotiating with North Korea, a fourth-rate power at best. Incredibly, it was the Koreans who set the pace—and it was an agonizingly *slow* tempo—in the lengthy negotiations. There was definitely patience in the negotiating methods used by the Koreans.

Having almost endless patience is a characteristic of Eastern cultures, a fact that became evident early during the Paris peace talks. The Americans stayed in a nearby hotel on a week-to-week basis. The Koreans, on the other hand, signed a two-year lease on a villa outside of Paris. The message this action conveyed to impetuous American negotiators eager to "get on with it" was this: "We're here to negotiate for as long as it takes. Don't expect to dazzle us with your superior military power."

But that's negotiation on the international level. Does the *patience* principle apply equally well to negotiations between companies and individuals? There's strong evidence that it does.

FORBEARANCE AS A FACTOR

When and where do you use *patience* as a negotiating tactic? It depends on a number of factors, but notably on how much forbearance *you* are capable of displaying. You should also consider whether the additional "time" created by using the technique is likely to work to your advantage.

For instance, a nationally known electronics firm decided to acquire a small manufacturer of highly specialized circuitry. The acquisition would have given the bigger company a state-of-the-art capability that otherwise would have taken many months to develop. In addition, it would have prevented their having to give up valuable floor space in their already cramped manufacturing facility.

Negotiators from the electronics firm approached the president of the small manufacturing company and made what appeared to be a generous offer. The offer included a sizable sum of cash, plus an option for the president of the smaller company to buy a large block of stock when it reached a certain level.

President Exhibits Negotiating Prowess

Negotiators expected the smaller company to accept immediately. But they had not reckoned on the president's negotiating ability. As it turned out, he not only knew how to use *patience* as a negotiating tactic, he also knew what most researchers on the subject have discovered: Quick negotiations almost always end up badly for one party or the other. In this case, the president of the smaller company figured—correctly as it turned out—that a hasty agreement might be to his *dis*advantage.

As a result, the president continued to put negotiators from the bigger electronics firm off, even under a mild threat of the bigger company withdrawing its offer. Meanwhile, the president of the smaller company did what a power negotiator should do in such circumstances. He used the extra time to check out assumptions he had made. One was that the bigger company had a great deal to gain from the acquisition, perhaps making his company more valuable to them than he had originally thought.

There's Risk Involved

There was a danger, of course, that the President could have been wrong in his assumption. In such a case, the bigger company would have probably withdrawn its offer and looked elsewhere. That's one of the risks of overdoing the patience routine.

In this case, however, the assumption proved to be valid, netting the smaller company about a half million more than the original offer. Patience paid off in this situation.

USING PATIENCE ON THE PERSONAL LEVEL

Using *patience* at the personal level often involves considering long-term rather than short-term rewards. "Winning" now means instant gratification, of course. Winning later obviously means postponing the reward. This is an important point to remember when using this technique.

For example, some years ago, an outstanding young athlete was wooed by several major-league baseball clubs after graduating from high school. One club offered him a large bonus—in the neighborhood of $75,000 as I recall it—to sign immediately.

The alternative course for the youngster was to accept a full athletic scholarship at a top-ranked four-year college. Thus the young man's choice narrowed down to a $75,000 bonus *now* versus a scholarship worth between $30,000 and $40,000. The reality, of course, was that the $75,000 would be in hard cash, while the scholarship would be an "intangible." In either case, the bonus represented an *instant* gain, while the scholarship promised a long-range benefit.

Did He Take the Right Course?

The young athlete showed remarkable patience in finally negotiating for the longer-range benefit. The jury is still out on which path would have produced the greater long-range benefits, but my guess is that he took the right course. With a college degree in hand, the youngster increased his chances of having greater earning power after finishing his baseball career. Another significant factor here is the average tenure of a professional athlete. It's short.

Negotiations for *established* professional athletes are another matter—one we'll discuss in some detail in a later chapter.

Suffice it to say that patience can be an effective technique when used at the right time and place.

Coping with the Technique

What is the antidote? How do you counter the patience technique when used by others on you?

You begin by taking a hard look at the other person's position—and motivation. Is the other party showing "legitimate" *patience*, or merely stalling—or outright bluffing? What does the other party have to gain—or lose—from using the tactic? What kind of effect would your withdrawal have on the negotiation? When does patience end and discretion begin? An in-depth analysis should reveal tentative answers to all these questions.

USING "IT'S-ALREADY-DONE" (FAIT ACCOMPLI)

My car wasn't running right, so I took it to a nearby garage to get it repaired. The mechanic couldn't spot the problem immediately, so he said he would call later if it was "something serious."

Since the mechanic didn't call, I arrived at the garage that afternoon expecting to get off with a fairly light bill. Instead, the mechanic tapped me for $192.35.

Naturally, I was upset. "I thought you were going to call," I said indignantly.

"Couldn't get in touch with you," the mechanic said. "Besides, you *had* to have the work done. You couldn't have driven another day with it like it was."

So what could I have done? *Fait accompli!* The deed had been done.

Using the Technique Sparingly

It's a tactic you'll want to use sparingly, if at all, for obvious reasons. Negotiating in good faith means talking it over with the other party, then taking action based on those discussions. *Fait accompli* essentially short circuits the negotiation process. You act first—negotiate *later!*

Few acts of *fait accompli* are as flagrant as the one perpetrated by my mechanic friend. (In fact, most mechanics I know are quite ethical in their operations and frown on this sort of activity.)

The main problem in using act-now-negotiate-later is that your opponent gets little, if anything, from the negotiation except for an *unwelcome surprise and a bruised ego.*

Using Modified Fait Accompli

There are ways to use *fait accompli* in a modified and more acceptable way, without "wiping out" the other party.

Printing, for example, can be a risky business. A bad typographical error can ruin an otherwise beautiful printing job. Multi-color printing jobs can be especially tricky. A slightly out-of-register press can mean the difference between a printing "masterpiece" and a botched printing job that usually has to be redone.

One big Southwest printer uses a modified *fait accompli* to handle jobs that are only slightly imperfect. Having detected a minor flaw, they send the job out to the customer anyway. It's a slightly calculated risk, but they take it for a couple of reasons.

Comes Out Slightly Ahead

In the first place, some customers don't catch the minor flaw at all and accept the order as is. Most do, however, and immediately call it to the printer's attention.

The printer apologizes profusely and agrees to redo the job. But in the same breath, he adds, "But you know, that flaw is so small it's hardly noticeable. We didn't even catch it till you called it to our attention. What do you say if I run the job as is for you at cost. It'll mean a substantial reduction in cost."

Some economy-minded customers go along with the idea; this placates the customer and saves the printer's having to do an expensive reprint. "Cost," incidentally, includes a little padding, so it turns out to be a slightly better than break-even proposition for the printer.

A Lender Uses the Technique

Another mild form of fait accompli is used by some mortgage companies, jointly with Realtors in most cases, on interest rates and discount points charged buyers and sellers.

Interest, of course, must be paid by the buyer on the loan he secures. "Points" are usually paid by the seller to the investor to make up the difference in interest rates between conventional and government-insured or guaranteed loans (FHA and VA). And since one discount point equals one percent of the loan, points can be an expensive item.

Both interest rates and discount points are based on *current* market conditions, which means either can fluctuate within a short period of time. Thus the lender usually quotes a tentative interest rate to the buyer, and tentative points as they prevail at that moment.

For example, a lender will tell a buyer or a Realtor "We should be able to get that loan for you at 9½ percent." Weeks later, the borrower is notified that his loan has just gone through—at 9¾ percent interest rate.

"What's the deal?" the buyer remonstrates.

"Couldn't help it," the lender responds, "The market changed yesterday."

The same thing happens quite often to sellers in paying discount points. At the time of sale, the lender or Realtor will quote, let's say, three discount points. Weeks later, when the deal is ready to close, he's informed that he'll have to pay four or five points, since the market has changed. It's all "legitimate," since the market *does* determine the rate.

Fait accompli—the deed is done!

Using the Technique Properly

Regardless of how legitimate the *fait accompli* might have been in these cases, you must use the technique with the greatest discretion. I would speculate that in these two cases, the buyer and seller might have willingly paid the higher interest rate and greater discount points *if* they were convinced the extra costs were necessary and fair. But if they doubted the validity of the increase, they would have been left in a vindictive mood. They would not have provided the word-of-mouth advertising needed to keep the Realtor and investor in business. Obviously, the technique should be used sparingly and with the greatest prudence.

Why a "Just" Fait Accompli Works

The bad part about *fait accompli* is that it creates unpleasant surprises for your opponent, and as a result—ill will. The "good" part, assuming the *fait accompli* is considered "just" by the other party, is that the other party usually resigns himself to the action rather quickly.

For instance, I recently bought a rather expensive sports coat at a fashionable men's store. I bought it for two reasons: it looked good and fit well, and it was being sold at one third off the original price.

When I received the bill a few days later, I was surprised to see that the store had charged me the full list price for the coat. I immediately called the store and protested. I even had my wife verify my story.

The salesman stuck to his story that the coat was never on sale, however, forcing me to threaten to send the coat back. But after I looked the coat over again, and tried it on, I was hooked. I decided to keep it anyway.

And so it is with a not-too-offensive *fait accompli*. Once the deed has been done and you have mentally accepted the new conditions, it becomes too much trouble to change things.

Defending Against the Tactic

As a power negotiator, you'll need to be able to defense this tactic when used against you.

One way is to go to the highest source of authority possible when you feel you've been "had." I realize now that I should have lodged my complaint against the store to the chairman of the board.

As the buyer in the real estate transaction, I should have had the originally quoted interest rate *written into the contract.* If you insist on it, few investors or Realtors will decline such a request.

The same would have held true for discount points. The seller should have had it written in the contract, or sales agreement, that he wouldn't pay over the points prevailing at that moment. This way, if the discount points go up before your home is sold, someone else will have to bear the financial burden. But it won't be you!

Perhaps the best defense against *fait accompli* is constant vigilance during the negotiation.

Chapter 4

THE THIRD MAN THEME: KEY TO POWER NEGOTIATING

As a power negotiator, you'll obviously want to handle most of your own personal and business transactions. At times, however, you can come out ahead by letting someone else negotiate for you—directly or indirectly.

Directly would be through a third party. Typically, this would be an expert—a literary or sports agent or a management consultant—who uses his knowledge and know-how to gain you advantages you probably couldn't have negotiated for yourself.

Negotiating *indirectly* is another matter. In this case, you do your own negotiating, all right. But you leave the actual decision making to a third party—real or *imaginary*. For example, a buyer might negotiate a price with a seller, only to discover belatedly that the seller must get "approval" from his sales manager (who again can be real or imagined).

NEGOTIATING WITH LIMITED AUTHORITY

This process is called negotiating with *limited authority*. At first blush, this technique seems to have no place in power negotiating. Actually, there are many cases where it would be to your distinct *advantage* to have limited authority.

Having limited rather than full authority helped the purchasing agent of a West Coast electronics firm to negotiate a lower-than-usual price for a big order of missile components. These were high-tolerance parts made by only a few of the firm's subcontractors.

The salesman worked hard to establish a fair price for the order. But the purchasing agent rejected the bid. "This is a big order," he told the salesman. "I feel we ought to get a bigger break on the price." This type of "price squeezing," incidentally, is not uncommon on big-ticket items.

The squeeze worked, since the salesman came up with a lower price the second time around. "Looks good," the purchasing agent said this time. "I'll let you know within the week."

"A week!" the salesman exclaimed. "Why not now? After all, I've given you my best shot."

"You're absolutely right," the agent replied, "and I appreciate it. However, on purchases of $100,000 and more, we have to get approval from the corporate office."

"I didn't know that," the salesman said. "Why didn't you tell me at the outset?"

"I'm sorry," the purchasing agent replied, "I thought you knew."

Benefits of Limited Authority

Having limited authority in the negotiation helped the purchasing agent in several ways.

First, it gave him additional time to evaluate the seller's bid, which *was* rather complicated.

Second, it gave him the option of seeking other bidders if he felt he might be able to get a better offer elsewhere.

Third—and perhaps this is the most important point of all—it gave the purchasing agent a chance to say "No" gracefully, had Corporate Office rejected the bid. In such an eventuality, the purchasing agent could have maintained a good working relationship with the salesman by complaining, "That Corporate Office bunch—they wouldn't recognize a good bid if they saw one!"

Byproducts: "Missing Man" and "Surprise"

The limited authority technique is an integral part of two other negotiating tactics which are fairly widely used. One is *surprise*, which we'll explore more fully in a later chapter. The other is *missing man*, a tactic sometimes used in higher-level negotiations.

For example, a Dallas developer was anxious to acquire a medium-sized mortgage company in order to establish an in-house lending capability. He hired an attorney—one who had a reputation for handling mergers and big business deals—to represent him in the negotiation.

The attorney received a number of prospective sellers from a "blind ad" he ran in leading trade journals and business publications. By careful screening, he narrowed the list down to three companies that seemed most likely to meet his client's needs.

Client Remains Anonymous

The lawyer then began preliminary negotiations with all three companies. He explained at the outset that he would do all the negotiating, but that his client—who would remain anonymous until the final discussions—would have to approve the final offer. Thus he appeared to set down clearly his limited-authority position.

Negotiations continued off and on for several months. The lawyer kept all three companies interested and was able to gain price concessions from all three.

Sensing that the prospective sellers were becoming anxious to close, the lawyer narrowed the bidding down to the two companies he thought would offer them the most.

Unfortunately, the owner of one of the companies (we'll call it Company A) insisted on an answer. "If you can't give us an answer right away," the owner insisted, "you can forget the whole deal."

"Ultimatum" Forces Action

The "ultimatum" *was* rather untimely, since the lawyer felt he was on the verge of negotiating a "super deal" with the owner of Company B.

Many negotiators would at that instant have taken the bird in hand (Company A) over the uncommitted bird in the bush (Company B). But the lawyer knew a thing or two about stalling; at this point he executed his missing-man game plan.

"I'll call my client right now," he told the owner of Company A. "May I use your phone?"

The lawyer "discovered" in the phone conversation that the developer was out of town, but could be reached at a downtown New York hotel. He called the hotel, only to discover that the developer had "just checked out," destination unknown, at which point the negotiating principals had to consider the developer "missing."

Stalling Tactic Pays Off

The owner of Company A was upset. However, the lawyer was able to convince him that the developer would almost certainly be in by Monday morning, at which time he would surely give an answer.

Meanwhile, the lawyer intensified negotiations with the owner of Company B, who finally agreed to the lawyer's asking price, a price better than Company A's.

When the developer returned to the office Monday morning, he promptly accepted Company B's offer. Thus the missing-man technique permitted the lawyer to negotiate the best possible deal for his client with minimal risk. And in the process, he was able to maintain a good relationship with all parties.

Using the missing-man technique is much like using the deadline tactic. Just as most people (in most situations) will accept your deadline as theirs, so they tend to accept your limited authority as real. And limited authority, you'll recall, can be either real or *imagined*.

Negotiating an Honorarium

For example, I once found myself negotiating a fee for a training seminar I had proposed for the members of a statewide trade association. Because the seminar would require considerable research, I suggested an honorarium slightly higher than the one I had previously charged the association.

"Sorry," the association executive director said, "but our new president says I can't go a penny higher than what we said before."

I reemphasized the fact that the project would require my doing heavier-than-usual research, which would justify the higher charge. Still, the director insisted the higher honorarium would have to be approved by the president of the association. And as fate would have it, the president was "out of town" and couldn't be located.

Limit Wasn't Real

The bottom line was: I did the work for the normal honorarium. "There's nothing I can do about it," I rationalized, "so why fight it?"

A few months later, however, I discovered quite by accident (through a secretary in the association) that I had been thoroughly outnegotiated. There *was* no limit on the honorarium the association could pay speakers, and the director—*not* the president—had full authority in such matters. What's more, the president was not out of town during this time frame.

Thus I had fallen into a trap many unsuspecting negotiators fall into. I assumed the other party did not have full authority to handle the transaction. Otherwise, it seemed to me, he would have told me so.

Unfortunately, I did not follow one of the basic principles of power negotiation: test your assumptions to make sure they're valid.

PINPOINTING THE DECISION MAKER

Polished power negotiators rarely make this mistake. For starters in almost any negotiation, they determine directly or indirectly if their opponent has *final* authority to make decisions. If the other party has full authority, they start negotiating in earnest. If not, they make a concerted effort to find out *where* the final authority lies and how to get that source involved, if at all possible, at the outset.

"My associates used to run into this limited-authority business all the time," said Jerry Sparks, a well-known Dallas Realtor. "They would carefully qualify a client and find him a home perfectly suited to his needs, only to have him say, 'It looks great, but we've got to get Uncle John's okay before we can buy. After all, he's putting down the down payment.'"

Qualifying a Buyer

"This rarely happens today, mainly I think because people ask this question in qualifying prospects: 'If we find the home you like today, will you be able to make the decision to buy yourself?' Then we know exactly where we stand."

Clearly, the best defense against having limited authority used successfully *against* you is to directly ask the other party if he or she has the final authority to handle the matter at hand. Make sure, in other words, that you're dealing with the real decision maker.

THE PRINCIPLE IN ACTION

Limited authority and its first cousin, missing man, are techniques used widely, though no doubt often unwittingly, in many workaday situations. For example:

Loan Officer: "I'd like to get you a lower interest rate on this loan, but this is all my loan committee will approve."

Bookkeeper: "I can't pay anything over $25 out of petty cash."

Supervisor: "I'd certainly like to give you a bigger raise, but the salary review committee has got my hands tied."

Real estate salesperson: "I've been trying to submit your offer for a week, but the owner is still out of town—somewhere!"

Professor: "I'd sure like to make an exception and give you a better grade, but the Dean has put his foot down on these matters."

Taxi Driver: "The company won't let me take fares to the airport."

Clerk: "I'm not authorized to exchange purchases of this type ma'm. You'll have to contact the home office in Boston."

Secretary: "I'd like to be able to give you an answer today, but my boss is out of town and I don't know for sure when he'll be back."

Boss: "My secretary handles all contributions. You'll have to get in touch with her."

Wife: "I'd like to give you an answer, but my husband handles all the books in our family."

Husband: "I'd like to give you an answer, but my wife handles the books in our family."

And so forth.

Saying "No" Gracefully

Used properly, limited authority is a powerful negotiating technique. It can buy you some time and allow you to say "No" gracefully, thereby allowing you to maintain a good working relationship.

Improperly used, it can destroy trust in future negotiations and make relationships strained. Use it discreetly.

USING MEDIATION FOR POWER LEVERAGE

Studies show that a third party can frequently influence negotiations greatly. This seems to be especially true in union-management negotiations, where stakes are high and negotiating usually takes place at both organizational and personal levels.

This idea was dramatized recently in negotiations between a U.S. aerospace conglomerate and the biggest of the seven unions with which it dealt.

Negotiating at Two Levels

Negotiation at the personal level was between Jake Wolanski, chief union negotiator, and Wallace Anderson, Vice President of Labor Relations for the aerospace firm. The two men were almost direct opposites in style, background, and temperament.

Jake was an ex-welder who joined the company shortly after graduation and soon afterward became union steward in his department. He then joined the union organization as a local representative, and over the years worked his way up to chief negotiator of his local. Jake was an impetuous, tough-talking negotiator who had a reputation for "sticking it to the company" when he could. He allegedly held a personal grudge against the company for being passed up for a foreman's job some years back.

Wallace joined the company after graduating from Harvard Law School. He was an articulate, patient negotiator who had a reputation as an indefatigable researcher. "You'd better do your home work when you go to the negotiating table with Wallace," one union leader said, "because it's a cinch he's done his."

Adamant on Main Issues

Early in the negotiations between the two, both sides made minor concessions. As time wore on, it became obvious that both were sticking to their guns on the really important issues. Briefly, here's what they were:

The company had proposed a 17 percent increase over the next three years. It had also offered to add several fringe benefits, including notably an extra paid holiday and an improved dental plan. The offer was in keeping with industry standards, and in some respects, ahead of it.

The union was asking for a 25 percent increase over three years. In addition, it was seeking even more generous health benefits, plus—and this turned out to be a surprise to the company—plantwide seniority rights. This meant that if a most senior employee were laid off in one department, he could transfer to another, regardless of his job classification. This could mean, for example, that an electrician with good seniority might end up in, say, the drafting department.

Management Has Its Say

Jake and Wallace negotiated skillfully and with apparent authority. In reality, however, their "authority" was somewhat limited. Both had the green light to make concessions, so long as they stayed within the general parameters set down by top management. And management kept a close surveillance.

The international union, for example, had its sights set on establishing the plantwide seniority clause. And headquarters made it plain to the local that they wanted to use the local union as a "testing ground." Thus this item was virtually nonnegotiable, though not so stated by the union.

Company officials, on the other hand, were somewhat "flexible" on fringe benefits. However, they were dead set against going over the 17 percent raise. Such a raise without added productivity would be ruinous, they claimed. The company had not taken a stand on the seniority issue, simply because they were not aware that the union was ready to make this demand. This, of course, reflected poor planning on the company's part.

These basic organizational demands on either side—the plantwide seniority clause and the 17-percent pay raise—

naturally affected the performance of both Jake and Wallace throughout the negotiation.

At one point, for example, Jake called Wallace an "overpaid egghead . . . incapable of understanding the real problems of the working man." Such intemperate accusations caused the usually unflappable Wallace to retaliate in kind. "You're a disloyal parasite who has absolutely no concern for the company's future," he fired back at one point.

These personal differences, coupled with the organizational restraints imposed on the two, ultimately led to a deadlock in negotiations. And at this point, there was really only one way to resolve the issue: bring in a third person—a disinterested, objective third party—whose findings would be binding on either side.

Pros and Cons of Mediation

Why was a mediator necessary? Mainly because neither of the negotiators could make a major concession without appearing to be "weak" and ineffective.

There are advantages—and certainly potential disadvantages—to having a third party resolve a negotiation.

One disadvantage at the personal level is that the authority of either negotiator is usurped entirely. In a sense, both have to admit "failure"; neither can emerge a clear-cut winner.

And there are other potential disadvantages. A mediator can hardly ever know the issues as well as the negotiators themselves. Further, the mediator does not have to *live* with the decision. For example, let's assume the mediator was to accept the union's plantwide seniority demand. Later, it will be some frustrated foreman who will bear the brunt of the decision. It will be he, not the mediator, who will have to make room for experienced but sometimes unqualified people in the department.

ADVANTAGES OF A THIRD PARTY

These disadvantages are, in many cases, outweighed by the advantages of having a *neutral* and highly qualified third party resolve the issue. Such a third party can:

• Compel both sides to make concessions they would not otherwise have made. Tests show conclusively that bargainers who agree to arbitration are generally willing to make larger—and more frequent—concessions than they would have made during regular negotiations themselves.

• Become a scapegoat of sorts for either side. After all, either side can claim, it was *he*, not *us*, who made the decision. This allows negotiators on either side to save that all-important "face."

• Reestablish communication between the negotiating parties. Often, when negotiations get down to name calling, communication breaks down completely, making resolution of the problem all but impossible.

Neutrality Is a Must

The "catch" to all this is that the third party must be scrupulously neutral. And of course he or she must be able to examine issues completely and render a fair decision. In labor cases such as the one just mentioned, the negotiating parties can turn to the American Arbitration Association for help. This organization maintains a list of highly qualified arbitrators who must be agreed upon by all parties.

People will normally negotiate, you'll recall, only if they feel there's something to be gained from the transaction. By the same token, two parties will normally agree to mediation only if they feel the third party will rule favorably for them on at least some of the important issues.

Both Sides Gain

Mediators recognize this fact and try to make certain both sides *do* gain some of their objectives.

In the case under discussion, the mediator ruled on a modified plantwide seniority plan—a significant concession. On the other hand, he kept the pay hike at 17 percent and disallowed fringe benefits which would have been potentially ruinous to the company.

By using a mediator, the aerospace conglomerate and the union avoided a strike, which would have been costly to both sides. And basic needs of both sides were met.

How Others Can Do It

In other situations, a third man can negotiate more successfully for you because he or she has greater knowledge and better contacts, which give that person far more leverage than you could have in negotiating for yourself.

We'll take a look at how a lawyer, a literary agent and a sports agent negotiated successfully for their clients in the next chapter.

Chapter 5

USING AN AGENT TO GAIN POWER IN NEGOTIATION

What course of action would you take if you were:

● The widow of an executive who was killed in a plane crash that might have been caused by either poor maintenance or faulty design—or both?

● A well-known writer trying to get a large advance for an unwritten novel?

● A proven professional football player trying to negotiate a healthy pay hike with a won't-budge management?

USING A THIRD PARTY

Chances are, you would come out ahead—in some cases, dramatically ahead—by hiring a competent third party, or agent, to negotiate *for* you.

If you are already a power negotiator, there might be circumstances under which you could successfully fend for yourself. But in certain cases, such as those mentioned above, it's likely the claimants would profit most by letting a bona fide expert pinch hit for them at the negotiating table. In fact, that's precisely what happened.

Why an Agent Can Net You More

An agent can normally do a better job than you can do for yourself when: (1) you're an individual fighting "city hall," or (2) when the negotiation requires a highly specialized body of knowledge.

Both conditions existed in large measure in each of these situations. Individuals were negotiating with "corporate giants." And in these cases the negotiation required in-depth knowledge of aviation law, the publishing business and professional football management. Expertise in such highly specialized fields is usually acquired only through years of experience.

And even if you are a power negotiator with specialized knowledge, there's an odds-on chance the agent can swing a better settlement than you can negotiate for yourself. We'll explore *why* in a moment.

Lawyer Ups the Ante

The widow of the aircraft disaster victim was one of 41 clients of a famous New York lawyer who specialized in aviation accident law. In each of the 41 cases, the insurance company tried to settle quickly for $58,000 apiece. The lawyer, after two years of negotiation, managed to win settlements of up to $650,000 for some of the clients.

Admittedly, the lawyer's fees were high: 17½ to 25 percent of the settlement. But even after paying the fee, most of the clients came out way ahead of the game. Why was the lawyer able to negotiate more? There were several key factors.

Why the Third Party Helped

First, his status as a lawyer, especially one steeped in aviation accident law (there just aren't many of this species around), undoubtedly carried great weight with the court. Too, judges tend to intimidate laymen who "masquerade" as lawyers.

Another highly reputed lawyer who specializes in aviation accident law can recall no case where such a victim or claimant benefited by dealing directly with a liability insurance company.

Second, only a legitimate expert usually knows how to arrive at an equitable settlement, mainly because he is able to calculate what the market will bear. He did so in this case by considering such factors as the victim's age, potential earning power and relationship to the claimant. Sure, an individual could arrive at a settlement figure. But based on what precedents?

And third, someone had to *prove* the airline or the plane manufacturer was at fault. Normally, this is a most difficult feat, even for the most highly skilled and knowledgeable attorney in the field.

USING THE TACTIC IN INSURANCE

My experience in insurance and real estate tends to confirm—in different ways—that an objective third party, an agent if you will, can negotiate more successfully for you than you can negotiate for yourself in many cases, perhaps most.

For example, during my brief stint as an insurance adjuster some years ago, I quickly learned that the company rewarded adjusters who could settle with the claimant quickly, particularly where it appeared the damage might be extensive. This was relatively easy to do in many cases because claimants generally subscribe to the bird-in-the-hand philosophy. They were more interested in a short-term reward than the prospect of a more substantial gain at some furute point in time. Looking back, I feel fairly certain a good number of these people could have gained substantially more in damages by going through a competent claims lawyer.

Where lawyers did intervene, they were able in many cases to negotiate settlements as much as several hundred percent above what the insurance company had initially offered. They were able to do so for the same reasons the aviation lawyer was able to negotiate huge settlements for the air crash victims.

USING THE TACTIC IN REAL ESTATE

I found the principle works as well in real estate, where sellers are often understandably reluctant to pay a six percent commission—or more—to have their home sold by a Realtor.

As a Realtor, I used to tell owners of more expensive properties, "Look, I can probably get you eight to nine percent more for your property than you can get selling it yourself—and save you all the headaches that usually go with such an effort."

Why could I frequently get more? Because I had the real estate knowledge and expertise a top-notch negotiator needs to handle such a transaction convincingly. Most sellers lack these prerequisites and negotiate poorly, mainly because they become subjectively involved in the transaction.

How to Use "Evidence" in Your Cause

To make my position convincing, I had to assume the role of devil's advocate. If I were in the seller's shoes, would *I* take *my* word for it that I could get eight or nine percent more (thus netting the seller two to three percent more, even after deducting the commission)? The answer was no, I wouldn't be convinced without some sort of "evidence."

Thus I employed the evidence technique, which is discussed in more detail in a later chapter. But briefly here's what happened. I showed them articles from two leading publications to support my claim. The first was a reprint from *Reader's Digest*, written by a homeowner who had moved many times, with and without a Realtor's services. His conviction: You can probably come out ahead, even if you use a Realtor.

The other was an article taken from the *Washington Post,*

another prestigious publication. It showed the results of a survey which concludes that a Realtor could, in fact, get eight to nine percent more on selling larger, custom-built homes, for reasons already mentioned.

HOW AUTHORS IMPROVE THEIR LOT

What do Norman Mailer, Spiro Agnew and Judith Campbell Exner have in common? They, among many others, retained literary agent Scott Meredith of New York City to negotiate with publishers for their unfinished works. And there is little doubt that Meredith was able to get each of these personalities more money than they could have negotiated for themselves—perhaps *considerably* more.

After leaving the White House in disgrace, Agnew contacted Meredith about a novel he was writing. Surprisingly, it was a work of fiction, *The Canfield Decision.*

The chances of a neophyte novelist landing a sizable advance are slim, even for a former Vice President But Meredith, who has been tagged "superagent" by his professional peers, was able to use his formidable negotiating prowess to swing a $250,000 price tag for serial rights to the work. Not bad for an untutored literary effort!

Lawyer Contacts Meredith

Meredith's relationship with Exner started with a phone call from still another third party—her lawyer. "Would you be interested," he asked Meredith, "in handling a book about Judith's affair with the late John F. Kennedy?"

Meredith had no illusions about the book becoming a literary masterpiece. However, he realized the tremendous public appeal of such "backstairs gossip." "I didn't feel such a book would do any real harm to the President's memory," he said. "You have to bear in mind that the President was a healthy young man who, for practical purposes, was separated from his wife. For political reasons, he chose to remain married. This book would simply point out that he was human."

Accordingly, Meredith pieced together a tantalizing 10-page outline previewing the work. He used this outline to sell rights for the book to the *National Enquirer* in the United States and to the *Daily Mail* in London for a tidy $300,000.

Meredith Uses "Old" Technique

But perhaps Meredith's most outstanding power negotiation was to get a flat $1 million for an unwritten Norman Mailer novel. His huge success in this transaction illustrates graphically how coupling extraordinary negotiating power with a creative approach can net outstanding results.

Creativity is not, as is popularly believed, thinking up something entirely new. It is simply substituting, adapting, or modifying existing ideas, products and services—or, to put it another way, it's putting an old idea into a new setting.

Auction Technique Breaks Tradition

For example, the *auction* technique of negotiating has been used with varying degrees of success for a long, long time. Literary agents have been around for a long time, too. And in general, they have been an ultraconservative group, dealing with publishers mainly on a gentlemanly one-on-one basis.

By and large, the good ones have done well by their clients. But it took a super power negotiator like Meredith to get record results. Here's how it happened in Mailer's case.

One publisher offered Meredith $750,000 for Mailer's *unwritten* novel. Incredibly, Meredith turned the offer down cold—a rejection which astounded the staid literary agency world. "Almost anyone would have jumped at the chance to land such a contract," one highly regarded agent said.

Ten Publishers Submit Bids

After rejecting this sizable offer, Meredith literally auctioned the book off. He sent 10 copies of a simple description of the book to 10 different publishers. He also used another power-negotiating tactic—a *real* deadline for submitting a *firm* offer.

This strategy enabled Meredith to negotiate a cool $1 million for Mailer's novel. Why does the auction technique work so well for Meredith? What's to prevent *all* publishers from turning in low bids? Probably for the same reason a valuable and highly coveted item will bring such a high price at a public auction: bidders' egos get involved. And when they do, the price goes up, causing the buyer to pay more than the item is probably worth.

Why the Tactic Is Justified

Is using the auction technique "fair?" Meredith, whose primary function is to get his clients the very best deal he can, thinks it is. "The author has probably spent a year or so in writing the book," he says, "and maybe another year or so in sending it around to publishers. By the end of the second year, the author is willing to take almost any kind of deal."

"Almost everyone in the business raised their collective eyebrows and called it a no-no when Meredith started using the auction technique," said one senior editor. "Now they're all imitating him."

Meredith's modus operandi appeals to scores of top authors, including Taylor Caldwell, Earnest K. Gann, Gerald Green, Arthur C. Clarke, Ellery Queen, Jessica Mitford, and Dr. Carl Sagan.

Used ethically, the auction tactic is a legitimate way to create competitive interest and establish a fair market price. Variations of the technique are used widely in the business world.

Realtor Creates Competitive Spirit

For example, Jim Whaylen, a successful Dallas Realtor, likes to create a competitive posture on highly saleable homes.

"Buyers usually like to put in a low offer on a home," he said, "and in many cases, they're justified in doing so. However, I've found that if a buyer really likes the home and feels someone else is interested, he will usually put in a higher offer."

The trick, of course, is to detect whether the prospect is *really* interested. It's unethical, of course, for a Realtor to tell one prospect what another prospect has offered for a home however, he *can* "show" them. For instance, Jim manages to arrange home showings so that one buyer arrives on the scene while another buyer is in the process of looking. If either of the prospective buyers feels the other is interested, one or both may submit an offer which is pretty close to list price.

Jim feels he can sometimes negotiate a higher offer by using such phrases as, "I'll see if the property is still available; we've had lots of people look at it today." Or, "I'm pretty sure a contract is being submitted on the home today. If you're really interested, we'll need to make our offer as attractive as possible."

"If you can convince the buyer the home is really up for grabs, he'll usually bid very competitively," Jim contends.

VARIATIONS OF THE TACTIC WORK

One businessman uses variations of the auction technique. On one occasion, he'll have several bidders wait in his reception room while he interviews them one at a time. On another, he'll have two or more companies put on presentations at the same time in separate rooms at his facility. And on still another, he'll "leak" prices submitted by other bidders. All such moves are aimed at negotiating a higher bid.

The auction technique is generally regarded as unethical when a shill is used. At a regular auction, for example, the "house" will plant a person, or persons, in the crowd to stimulate bidding. Such tactics are generally frowned on in ethical business transactions. Power negotiators must learn to detect and defend themselves against the shill.

Herrera and the Dallas Cowboys

The professional football player mentioned at the outset is Efren Herrera, former placekicker for the Dallas Cowboys' professional football team. When his contract expired, Herrera held out for a quantum salary increase.

Cowboy management offered him a flat 50 percent raise. Herrera turned the offer down; however, the Cowboys remained firm on their offer, creating an impasse.

Woy Enters the Picture

It was at this juncture that Herrera signed up with William (Bucky) Woy, a Dallas-based agent/consultant who has a reputation for negotiating big deals for sports stars.

"We decided that Herrera would either get what we were asking, or sit out the season," Woy insisted.

That's a pretty strong position to take against a power organization like the Cowboys, but the strategy worked. Within 48 hours, Woy had Herrera signing a contract with Seattle for *twice the salary he was making with the Dallas organization.*

How Did He Do It?

How did Woy negotiate successfully with the sophisticated Cowboy organization? By following the formula that has enabled him to land some of the most lucrative contracts for his clients in sports history.

That formula, simply stated, is to: research the issues thoroughly, develop a game plan for the negotiation, and almost always stick with the plan.

In Herrera's case, Woy found that his client had signed a three-year contract somewhat reluctantly with the Cowboys at a figure below the league norm for placekickers. "The Cowboys told him they would take care of him later on if he performed well," Woy said. "Well, Herrera did an outstanding job. For three years he was one of the better placekickers in the National Football League. And for sheer ability, he was probably the worst-paid kicker in the league."

Game Plan Works

Armed with these convincing facts, all substantiated by research, Woy evolved his game plan. Hold out to the bitter end for dollar goals, and at the same time seek an NFL club in need of a top-notch placekicker. It's almost impossible to contend in pro football without a competent placekicker.

The plan worked. Within 48 hours, Woy had negotiated a new contract for his client with Seattle at twice what Dallas was paying him. What's more, his new location would improve Herrera's chances of getting commercials in the Los Angeles and San Diego areas, where he is quite popular with fans.

CONFIDENCE LEVEL IS HIGH

Certainly part of Woy's success can be attributed to his high expectation level. "Sure, I'm confident when I go into a negotiation," said the erstwhile pro golfer, "but that confidence is based to a large extent on my having done my home work. Preparation is the name of the game."

Woy needs a high aspiration level, for in many of his negotiations, he has been the pronounced "underdog." For example, one of his most famous clients is Bob Horner, who at age 22 is one of the highest paid young superstars in organized baseball.

Horner signed with Woy shortly after graduating from Arizona State, where he was a baseball All-American. Woy negotiated one of the biggest deals on record for Atlanta's number one draft choice—a whopping $162,000 in bonuses, but that was only the beginning.

Huge Salary Asked

Horner had a spectacular rookie year, which was admittedly only a partial season. He led the club in home runs and runs-batted-in. Based on this performance, Woy was prepared to "shoot the moon" in negotiating Horner's salary during his sophomore season with the Braves.

Atlanta could have paid Horner as little as $21,000 in salary by league rules, but was of course prepared to pay much more. What they were *not* prepared to pay was Woy's seemingly exorbitant demand for $146,000, unprecedented for a second-year performer at that time.

Atlanta vs. Woy

Atlanta's position: Horner did, indeed, have a fine freshman season. Still, he was only in his second year in organized baseball, and he was asking for a salary normally reserved for superstars who had been around the league for five to ten years. After all, he *was* just barely out of college and hadn't yet "paid his dues." Most baseball players have to earn their spurs in the minor leagues.

Woy's case: Horner played baseball at Arizona State, a "baseball school" that plays as many as 100 games a year. Thus he was a highly seasoned "rookie" who, indeed, had earned his spurs before coming to the major leagues, and his salary ought to be based on *production*, not on precedent or his client's age.

The negotiation was long and bitter, finally ending in arbitration. Woy's rationale was apparently convincing, since arbiters decided in his client's favor.

Woy Is Pacesetter

"I don't believe in going by precedent," Woy said. "I believe in *setting* it. That's what makes the difference between myself and a lot of other people in this business."

For example, linebackers traditionally are not the highest paid players in professional football. Woy reversed this trend to a degree when he negotiated a several year, $1.2 million contract for Jack Lambert with the world champion Pittsburgh Steelers.

"Here again," Woy said, "I went by production—what the player was contributing to his team. And Lambert is not only one of his team's leading tacklers, he's an inspirational leader on the field."

Planning Is Essential

Again, Woy is convinced that research is the basis of effective negotiation. To prove his point, he can reel off facts and figures about salary structure and other relevant facts on virtually every major sports organization in the country. And when he needs specialized knowledge, he hires only top talent to get the proper expertise.

"After getting the facts, it's planning that counts," Woy said. "I've been in sports all my life and everything I do is geared to a game plan. I stick with this plan, and eventually it's like water going over a rock. I get where I want to be."

Part of this planning is a "dress rehearsal" in which Woy plays devil's advocate. "I tell my client what I'm going to say," Woy said, "and then I try to second-guess how the opposition is going to respond. This is a good way to cut down on surprises, which can hurt you in the real negotiation."

BUSINESS ACUMEN HELPS

Woy feels that he can negotiate a better deal for any sports star than that performer can negotiate for himself. One of the prime reasons, he asserts, is his business acumen. He has a deep knowledge of money management, tax shelters, deferred payments and other financial affairs. He also has been highly successful at working his clients into lucrative television commercials.

For instance, some years ago, Cadillac automobile was looking for a sports celebrity to appear in a series of ads. "I suggested Ben Hogan," Woy said, "because of something I had read in his book. Hogan said he was nearly killed when his car collided with a bus in the Texas Panhandle. He said the only thing that saved him was the fact that he was driving a Cadillac." Needless to say, Cadillac bought the idea immediately.

Other "Names" Use Woy

Other well-known commercial match-ups have included Lee Trevino and Dodge (the good guys), and Julius Boros and Lincoln automobile. It was Boros, incidentally, who encouraged Woy to launch his career as an agent.

Other notables represented by Woy, one way or the other, have included Joe Greene, Orville Moody, Roger Staubach, Ted Kwalick, Cedrick Hardman and Lee Elder.

Woy believes "watching and listening" are also vital steps in negotiation—points we'll explore further a little later. "Absolute honesty is important, too," he said. "If you tell the truth, you don't necessarily have to have a good memory."

Chapter 6

TACTICS AND TECHNIQUES FOR HANDLING THE QUESTION OF MONEY AND PRICING

Ralph LaPlante, Labor Relations Chief for a Midwest manufacturer, had been negotiating at length with union representatives.

The union had turned down flat the company's first offer, which called for a 7 percent wage hike, plus additional fringe benefits. Union negotiators were holding out for a whopping 15 percent pay increase and even more fringe benefits than the company had offered.

Negotiations continued back and forth in this vein for several days, with each side making minor concessions. Finally, they agreed on the benefits package, but they remained some distance apart on the wage increase.

"Final" Offer Submitted

At this point in the negotiation, Ralph received instructions from his corporate office: "Don't go over 10 percent, whatever the union threatens to do." Ralph immediately passed this word on to union negotiators. "The company has examined all issues thoroughly," he said, "and we feel 10 percent is as high as we can possibly go."

Though Ralph phrased his message quite diplomatically, he nonetheless said, in effect, "Ten percent is our final offer. *Take it or leave it*."

Fortunately for the company, the union "took it."

The technique used in this instance by Ralph LaPlante is one frequently employed in negotiations at virtually all levels—from personal to corporate. Appropriately, the tactic is called *take-it-or-leave-it*.

HOW AND WHEN TO USE THE TACTIC

It *can* be an effective negotiating technique, depending entirely on *how* and *when* it's used.

How should it be used? Diplomatically and matter-of-factly, rather than as a threat. The exact words, "Take it or leave it," should be used sparingly, if at all. Why? Because the phrase can—and usually *is*—intimidating. I have seen negotiators on the verge of agreement back off entirely when this phrase was used in negotiations, simply because they regarded it as a threat or ultimatum.

When should take-it-or-leave-it be used? In most cases, *after* the negotiation process has taken its full course, with each side having explored the issues in true give-and-take fashion. *Timing*, in negotiation as in almost any other endeavor, is of the essence. Ralph managed to use the tactic in a very timely way with the union.

When used as a not-too-thinly-disguised threat, take-it-or-leave-it can have negative results. When used like this, the technique is synonymous with a technique which many negotiators have come to call *Boulwarism*.

How Boulwarism Worked at GE

Lemuel R. Boulware was formerly head of labor relations for General Electric. He used the take-it-or-leave-it technique with perhaps unprecedented success in his negotiations with the company's several unions between 1947 and 1969.

A meticulous researcher, Boulware would carefully compile the company's wage and benefits package, based on productivity and other economic factors. Considerable "internal negotiation" ensued before Boulware was able to get approval from his top management, but once Boulware was able to get this agreement, he took a firm position. "We've worked this package out carefully," he told union negotiators, "and this is the best possible deal we can offer you. Take it or leave it."

The company was willing to negotiate some finer points of the package within the general limits set by Boulware, but almost never went beyond these limits.

The tactic worked surprisingly well for nearly 20 years especially during the period of relative economic stability following World War II.

Why the Technique Ultimately Failed

Ultimately, however, the tables were turned. The 13 unions working with General Electric got together in a long and costly strike.

Boulwarism eventually failed mainly, experts think, because the technique precludes meaningful negotiation. In fact, the term is now used sometimes in a derogatory sense to show that one party is not negotiating in good faith—not satisfying the needs of the other party.

Not that unions don't use the same tactic, albeit in a different way. For example, when a union threatens to call a strike by a certain date if their conditions are not met, they are in effect using take-it-or-leave-it.

Avoiding the Tactic at the Outset

Take-it-or-leave-it can be an ethical and effective power negotiating tactic, when used at the right time and place. Used inappropriately, however, it can negate a meaningful negotiation.

As a rule of thumb, you can say that take-it-or-leave-it is generally *not* effective when used at the outset of negotiations; this generally precludes effective dialogue over the issues.

When It Will Work

It can be effective when used after you have made appropriate assumptions about the opposition; after you have had a meaningful discussion of the issues; usually after you have gained some degree of leverage in the transaction; normally after you feel you are reaching an impasse; and invariably after you feel capable of using take-it-or-leave-it in a matter-of-fact rather than a threatening manner.

For example, here are some ways take-it-or-leave-it can be used "legitimately":

Buyer says to the seller: "That's as high as I'll be able to go under my present budget."

A client says to his lawyer (who wants the case as much for prestige as for money): "I'm sorry, that's about as much of a fee as I can stand. Otherwise, I guess I'll just have to get myself another lawyer."

The buyer says to the seller (who hasn't had a legitimate offer on his home in two months): "That's as high as I can possibly go. If you can't accept this offer, I guess I'll just have to start browsing through the multiple-listing book again."

The professional football or basketball standout (who realizes he's a "franchise"): "Well, if you can't go any higher than that, I guess I'll just have to put myself on the market as a free agent."

HOW TO USE (ONLY RARELY) AND COPE WITH LOWBALLING

If you're like me, buying a new car—or an old one for that matter—can be an exasperating experience.

The main problem, I think, is that there doesn't appear

to be a "standard" price for automobiles. If you go to five different dealers, you're likely to get five different prices—on the same model car! More often than not, there'll be a dramatic difference between the lowest and the highest price quoted.

The reason for this difference is a negotiating technique called *lowballing*. It's used frequently in the auto industry, and elsewhere too, in a modified fashion. Here's how it was used on us the last time we bought a car.

The Technique in Action

Like many buyers, my wife and I had a hard time deciding on the style and price car we wanted. After weeks of searching, we *finally* decided on *the* model we wanted.

Then the "fun" began in earnest. We went to five different dealers and insisted in each case on their giving us a *firm* price.

The prices quoted by four of the dealers were pretty well in line. But the fifth dealer was significantly lower (about 15 percent) than the others. "We're in luck," my wife said. "Not only did the dealer quote us the lowest price, but he has the color we want *in stock*. We won't have to wait like we would have had to do at the other dealers."

Delighted at the turn of events, we returned to the low bidder. Rather eagerly, I'm afraid, we announced that we were ready to buy. But our joy was short-lived.

Salesman Ups the Price

The dealer's tactic followed the traditional lowballing pattern. Quote a price low enough to get the buyer "hooked," then raise the price once he's committed to buying. Like most practitioners of the technique, he gave me a "logical" reason for the increase—a "mistake" on the appraiser's part. Other common excuses for raising the price might be: "We didn't include the extras"; or, "My sales manager overruled me; he says we'll lose money at the price I quoted you"; or, "I made a mathematical mistake in figuring the deal. Sorry about that."

Why the Tactic Is Used Sparingly

The lowballing technique lends itself to situations such as buying a car, where it is difficult to put a price on the commodity. However, salespeople for most "name" dealers use the technique sparingly today for several reasons.

For one thing, a more sophisticated buying public tends to be more aware of such tactics. And quite obviously, lowballing isn't a technique that's calculated to win friends and influence buyers to return as regular customers. Further, customers victimized by lowballing generally fail to provide the valuable word-of-mouth advertising most businesses need to stay in business. There's also the possibility—not too remote—that the customer will become irate and walk away from the deal.

We didn't walk away from the car dealer, however, and probably for the same reason many others don't. We had made a mental commitment to buying the car we had shopped so long and hard to find. As my wife so succinctly put it, we just wanted to "get this mess over with."

Lowballing, when used purposely to deceive, is a dubious technique at best. It is basically dishonest, and usually leaves the other party feeling unhappy and vindictive. Obviously, it should be used with the greatest care.

When Lowballing Is Acceptable

However, lowballing can—and often is—used in a subtle and generally more acceptable manner in business circles. For example, companies sometimes use the tactic to "buy in." They purposely submit a low bid to get the business, then escalate prices after they get their foot in the door. This situation is not without merit, especially when you have a top quality service or product to offer.

For example a well-established Dallas contractor found himself unable to land a contract for state-sponsored projects, though he bid repeatedly for the business.

Frustrated, the contractor sought advice from an outside consultant. Together, they mapped out a strategy that involved "buying in," which again is a more sophisticated form of lowballing.

"Justifying" His Action

In his own mind, the contractor "justified" his action. He knew his workmanship to be of the highest quality; the only reason he was not getting state business was because his bids were too high, and the state had a habit of almost always accepting the lowest bid.

He compared his plight to the astronaut's, whose dominant thought when sitting atop that million-dollar missile about to be blasted off into space was, "Just think, this beast is composed of 50,000 parts, all purchased from the cheapest bidder."

This contractor was a high bidder for several reasons. He always used top quality materials. He was a perfectionist who insisted on the very best workmanship, and he usually was conservative in his cost estimates. Many of the contractors whose bids were being accepted were just the opposite in the way they operated.

Consultant Suggests Switch

The consultant suggested a change in strategy. "If you can't whip city hall," he said, "why not join them? Put in a low bid next time, even if it means only making a marginal profit, or maybe even breaking even on the project. Once they see the kind of work you do, you're bound to get more business, even if your bid is higher."

It worked. The contractor landed a fair-sized contract and, as expected, made only a small profit. But he earned an instant reputation with the state as a quality contractor. As a result, his subsequent bids, even when high, got the state's attention. Today, his backlog of business usually includes a number of state projects.

Technique Widely Used

The buy-in technique, in its variations, is used almost universally. Department and grocery stores, for example, lure customers into their stores by offering a few brand-name products at much-lower-than-usual prices. Such "leader" items are often sold at cost—or under. But above-average charges are often charged for most other items in the store.

A large Southwest printer who does well-above-average work on expensive color brochures demands an above-average price. But in order to convince reluctant potential customers of his craftsmanship, he must sometimes "buy in." After these customers get accustomed to his quality work, they're "hooked." Then he can demand his regular prices.

Why does the technique work so well? "Because it's hard to go back to hamburger steak," he said, "once you've had a taste of filet."

America's giant aerospace firms, consciously or subconsciously, must use the buy-in technique almost continually. It is par for the course for most of these firms to have over-runs—sometimes *huge* overruns—on government contracts. The problem is compounded of course by the fact that they are dealing with state-of-the-art advances in technology, which makes price hard to figure in the first place. We'll discuss this problem more a little later.

Making Sure You're Not Victimized

How can you be sure you're not the victim of a well-conceived lowball strategem? You usually can't for certain. But you can *minimize* the possibilities by severely questioning almost any "good deal" you're offered.

If the price quoted you by another party seems un-reasonably low, ask quite candidly, "How can you do it for this price?"

If he gives what appears to be a sound explanation, and seems sincere, have him put it in writing. Then you'll know it's for real.

GAINING POWER THROUGH ESCALATION

First cousin to lowballing is a negotiating technique called *escalation*. Used ethically, it's an effective tactic—one every power negotiator ought to have in his arsenal. Used with an ulterior motive in mind, it can be as damaging to your cause as indiscriminate lowballing.

Like most popular negotiating stratagems, escalation can be used at all levels of human intercourse. Hitler, you'll recall used the tactic with signal success in negotiating with Chamberlain. At first, he asked for only a small chunk of Czechoslovakia—namely the part with a large German population. England agreed. But when Chamberlain flew half way across the continent to negotiate the transaction, Hitler escalated his demands; he wanted to take over the whole country. By the time negotiations ended, the Allies were elated to exchange *all* of Czechoslovakia for "peace for our time."

Negotiating to Build a Home

The technique seems to work best in business affairs where issues are not clearly defined and opposing parties are somewhat uncertain of their goals.

For example, a friend of mine once got an "informal" estimate from a contractor to build him a home. As a matter of fact, the contractor gave a "ball-park figure" of $70,000 over a couple of highballs.

My friend told the contractor his price was too high and that seemed to be the end of the negotiation. After shopping around a bit further, my friend began to see what a good deal the contractor had offered in the first place, whereupon he changed his mind and decided to accept the contractor's "offer."

When negotiations began in earnest, the contractor changed his tune. He set a *firm* price of $75,000. "After all," he explained, "I could give you only a ball-park estimate at the time. As you know, building costs have gone up quite a bit since we first talked."

"A Deal's a Deal"

All this was true, of course, and the increased price seemed to be "justified," but my friend couldn't see it that way. "After all," he stammered, "a deal's a deal."

The contractor finally agreed to his original $70,000 price tag, but at the same time got permission to eliminate a few frills.

Because the price escalation worked successfully, my friend was absolutely delighted to pay a price that only a few months earlier he had considered exorbitant.

This is how a power negotiator can make escalation work properly. He can make the other party actually feel good about a proposition that at first seems out of the question.

Actually, both the contractor and my friend profited in this transaction. The builder, by cutting some corners, was able to make his usual profit. The buyer saved face because he drove a hard bargain and held the contractor to his word.

ESCALATION IN REAL ESTATE

Escalation is a technique that readily lends itself to the property management phase of real estate, and in a very ethical way.

For example, if you are a landlord negotiating a lease on your property, you'll need to find some way to protect yourself from the ever-increasing taxes and the burgeoning cost of maintaining your property.

The energy crisis is creating still another "cost crisis" for landlords. In the southwest, for example, many landlords are now negotiating leases which allow them to charge extra if offices are kept open beyond the normal closing time and on weekends.

Defending Against Escalation

Such charges are justified in most cases. However, if you are negotiating as the occupant or lessee, you'll need to make certain that escalation clauses are not used *against* you.

For example, in negotiating a lease for a space in a New York office building, one unsuspecting lessee agreed to pay additional taxes calculated on a "base year." The base year, according to the lease, was considered to be the first 12-month period in which the lease commenced.

Unfortunately, he was one of the first occupants and total occupancy did not exceed 50 percent the first year. Thus his subsequent rent increase was based on the 50 percent occupancy rate rather than the 100 percent rate which prevailed the following year, and he ended up paying substantially more than his pro rata share of the taxes.

Keeping a Constant Vigil

A power negotiator should maintain a constant vigil against such inequities, whether they are purposely or accidentally committed by the other party.

He should be especially wary of clauses which base increases on such ambiguous phrases as "various consumer price indexes," or "significant changes in the economy," and so forth.

The best way to protect yourself against escalation is to obtain expert advice before negotiating a lease—or any other major document for that matter.

There are several other techniques commonly used in negotiating matters of money and pricing, and we'll discuss these in later chapters.

But these three—take-it-or-leave-it, lowballing, and escalation—are among the most frequently used. Learn when and how to use them expertly, and by all means learn to defend yourself against them as a power negotiator.

Chapter 7

GAINING NEGOTIATING POWER THROUGH ASSOCIATION

Pick up almost any popular magazine and you get the message: a movie star drives a certain make car; an all-pro linebacker smokes a name-brand cigarette; a business tycoon uses the services of a nationally known investment firm; and so forth.

What is the result of this seemingly endless procession of "testimonials?" In most cases, people buy these products in droves. Why? Because they like to *associate* with "winners."

USING THE ADVERTISER'S FAIL-SAFE TECHNIQUES

Association "works" because it allows you to join up with a person or issue or thing that you can relate to, however remotely. Birds of a feather *do* flock together, and if you're shrewd, you can use this principle to help improve your position as a power negotiator.

I'm suggesting that in negotiating with others you learn to use the "association" tactics practiced routinely by advertisers and public relations propagandists. Ray Dodson did and profited immensely.

Dodson is a veteran real estate dealer. He earned his spurs, so to speak, in residential sales. Later, he became active—and successful—in commercial real estate, but not without growing pains.

Transition Was "Rough"

"The transition from residential to commercial activity was rough, especially at the outset," Dodson said. "I think one of the main reasons was because sellers of residential property usually accept a flat fee commission schedule, while sellers of commercial real estate do not, especially on bigger deals. Worst of all, they would almost always try to reduce the amount of my commission, and in some cases eliminate it altogether!"

Lawyer Aids Cause

Finally, Dodson got an idea: why not bring his *own* attorney to the really big closings. He did and with positive results. "The fact that I had teamed up with an attorney seemed to make an instant impression," Dodson noted. "Together, we were able to stay right in the thick of negotiations. I seldom lost a commission after that, and I didn't have too many reduced."

The association worked so well, in fact, that Dodson and his lawyer eventually teamed up in commercial real estate and allied businesses. And so it is in many business ventures. Individuals with limited or marginal negotiating powers on their own become power negotiators when they join forces with a more formidable negotiating force.

GETTING A FIRM TO RELOCATE

For example, a representative of the Fort Worth Chamber of Commerce was negotiating with a New York-based firm which was planning to relocate "somewhere in the Sun Belt."

Competition was keen. Representatives from most major Sun Belt cities—including nearby Dallas—were offering all sorts of inducements to get the firm to relocate in their area.

But the Fort Worth representative knew a thing or two about how the association tactic can work in power negotiating. His research revealed that the chief decision maker for the New York firm was a former Syracuse football player who had performed against Texas Christian University, located in Forth Worth, some years back.

Football Star's Help Sought

Realizing this, the Fort Worthian immediately contacted a local businessman who had played on the TCU team against the New York decision maker's alma mater. "I think you can help yourself and your community, too," he told the ex-TCU star, "if you'll make the trip to New York with me, all expenses paid."

The TCU ex agreed. And though he played a relatively minor role in the actual negotiations, he did manage to swap stories with the firm's decision maker about that classic TCU-Syracuse gridiron struggle.

Generally, the firm's ultimate decision to locate near Forth Worth surprised almost everyone. But not the Fort Worthian, who knew the power of "associative" negotiating.

THE OTHER SIDE: DISASSOCIATION

Using association as a negotiating technique will generally succeed in direct proportion to the time and care spent in selecting an associate. Conversely, selecting the "wrong" partner (a tactic known as *dis*association) can be counterproductive. One case illustrates both sides of the coin.

A few years ago, two major aerospace companies were competing for a multipurpose fighter plane contract. Competition was intense, since the plane would likely provide the biggest contract to be awarded by the Air Force in the foreseeable future.

The plane was designed so that, with minor modifications, it could be used by both the Air Force and the Navy. This meant that the prime contractor would have to build mainly for the Air Force. In turn, this company would have to select a partner—a major subcontractor—to build the Navy version of the airplane.

Selecting a Subcontractor

Company "A" selected a subcontractor that had built many Navy fighter planes, dating back to World War II. This company was generally conceded to have a very good reputation with the Navy.

Company "B" selected a subcontractor with equally high credentials—until recently! What Company "B" failed to uncover in its investigation of its partner was the fact that the partner had *recently* fallen into disrepute with certain high-ranking Navy officers because of cost overruns and poor workmanship.

Both companies worked long and hard to design a plane with enough common parts (it's called *commonality*) to satisfy both the Air Force and the Navy. And both, in fact, turned out excellent proposals.

The selection committee, comprised of both civilian and service representatives, agonized at length over the decision, but finally selected Company "B," mainly because its version—at least on paper—had greater range and a bigger bomb-load capacity, and it was a trifle cheaper.

Secretary Reverses Decision

In a surprising move, however, the Secretary of Defense reversed the selection committee's decision and awarded the contract instead to Company "A." The reason, he said, was because Company "A" had greater commonality. Perhaps this *was* the main reason for the switch.

Insiders, however, insisted another factor entered the decision. They claimed Company "A" was given the contract mainly because of its association with a highly regarded Navy subcontractor. Or, to put it another way, Company "B" lost because of its affiliation with a less-liked subcontractor. *Disassociation*!

TACTIC WORKS IN PERSONAL AFFAIRS

The tactic of enlisting an associate with complementary expertise is commonly used in business and industry. But the technique can be used just as effectively in your personal life. Many use the association technique to improve their personal negotiating effectiveness, both at home and at the office. Jack Smith is a case in point.

Jack was a promising, but obscure young accountant in a big corporation. Like most "recruits" in the business world, Jack ranked relatively low in the pecking order. Thus he had little leverage in negotiating raises and promotions, and in getting his position accepted on important company issues.

Jack Gains Acceptance

It didn't take long, however, for Jack to become accepted as a "real comer" in the organization. He improved his negotiating position by observing—and later emulating—successful executives and associates around him. "They improved their position by hooking onto someone else's coattail," he said, "Why couldn't I?"

So Jack methodically selected the "associates" who he felt would most likely be able to help him improve his position. His first selection was his boss, an obvious choice because of the influence he had on Jack's career path. He worked his way into the boss's tennis club, became a substitute in his bridge club, and was frequently seen with him on coffee breaks and on other social occasions.

This was just enough association to encourage others in the office to conclude—only partially correctly in this case—that Jack was now a member of the office inner circle.

Power Must Be Perceived

How did this belief give Jack leverage in negotiating? Well, whenever a controversial issue arose in the office, Jack didn't have to inject his own opinion. Because of his known association with his superior, he could simply say: "Well, here's how the boss feels about it . . ."; or perhaps, "The boss says that . . .", and so forth. He becomes, in effect, "his master's voice."

Actually, Jack was not all that entrenched with the boss. But again, based on appearances, the office staff *thought* he was. And remember: power exists only so long as it is perceived by others.

Picking Peer Associates Is Difficult

There's nothing especially new about enlisting the support of your boss. "Brown-nosing," as it's popularly called around the office water cooler, has been going on for a long, long time. What normally *does* require some skill is the ability to select *peer* associates who can successfully complement your negotiating capability.

There's usually some guess work in determining what peers to associate with. After all, how can you tell who will eventually move up in the organization? However, as a rule of thumb, one should obviously select people who you know or suspect to be in the boss's very good graces, and those who hold, if not the key spots in the organization, at least spots which have a high visibility.

Jack selected two peer associates for these very reasons.

Bright Youngster, Secretary Selected

One was a bright, affable recent college graduate. But there were a lot of young faces to choose from. What was more important in this case was that the young man had graduated from the boss's alma mater and belonged to the same fraternity. School ties can be important here, as can social and religious affiliations.

The other associate Jack selected was the boss's secretary of long standing. True, the secretary's name did not appear on the company's organizational chart; still, she carried plenty of clout. Like many executive secretaries, she determines when you can see the boss, or for that matter, *if* you can see him. Once you're "in" with the boss's secretary, everyone seems to know it—and negotiate with you accordingly.

These types of people show up in almost any office "in group." Your association with these inner-circle people will make others pay attention to you and what you have to say. Ultimately, this will help make you a power negotiator.

MARRIAGE: A SUSTAINED NEGOTIATION

Even in marriage, which might well be the most sustained negotiation many engage in, association can often net excellent results. Negotiable issues arise daily. For example: where will we vacation this year, the mountains or the beach? Where will we build that new house, in the valley or on a hill? What kind of car will we buy, a sports model or a four-door? What's for dinner, filets or hamburgers? Will the children attend public or private school? What church will we join? Ad infinitum! The list of negotiable marital items is virtually endless.

Marriage partners most commonly gain negotiation leverage through two types of "associates": their children, and if there are no children, through relatives and friends. A couple of brief cases illustrate the point.

Gary Is Outnegotiated

Gary and Linda couldn't agree on where to spend their vacation. Gary preferred a skiing trip to the mountains, insisting that such an excursion would be something "new and exciting." Linda, on the other hand, held out for a Caribbean cruise. But she did not champion her cause alone. Weeks before the decision was to be made, she enlisted the support of the couple's two teen-age daughters. She did so by selling them on the romantic nature of the cruise and by painting a word picture of how great they would look when they returned with a midsummer tan.

In the end, Gary was outnumbered and outnegotiated, thanks to the association technique.

Gaining Mother-in-Law Support

Jim and Shirley had no children, so their associates turned out to be friends and relatives. The negotiable issue here was whether Jim should take a position with his company's home office in New York.

Jim was excited about the possibilities of promotion and the potential challenge the new job could offer. Shirley didn't want to leave her family and friends in Tulsa. Thus fairly early in the negotiating game, Shirley was able to convince Jim's mother of the disadvantages of moving. She must have done a super selling job, for when it came time to negotiate the move, it was Jim's mother—*not* Shirley—who managed to put up the strongest argument against the move.

THIRD PARTY CAN BE OBJECTIVE

This is another advantage of selecting a strong and articulate associate to aid your cause. On occasion, you will be able to stand aside and let that third party negotiate *for* you. And quite often, he or she can be more effective by being more objective in the negotiation.

No doubt, selecting the right kind of associate can enhance your position as a power negotiator. Selecting the wrong party (diassociation) can work against you.

Chapter 8

MAKING PROPAGANDA
PAY OFF
IN POWER NEGOTIATING

A progressive Realtor who was trying to negotiate the movement of a Northern manufacturing plant to Dallas claimed that the average price of a home in his city was only $48,000.

The business development director of the same city's Chamber of Commerce sang quite a different tune in trying to lure a high-fashion department store to the city. He asserted the average price of a home in Dallas was $78,000.

And still another Dallas firm, a mortgage banker, informed its would-be investors, a conservative group by nature, that the average price of a home in the city was somewhere in between, roughly $63,000.

All Use Propaganda

All three parties negotiated successfully by using propaganda tactics that have long been an integral part of persuading others to your point of view.

Simply stated, propaganda is the act of disseminating

information which is likely to enhance your position or get your point of view across in a negotiation. This information is normally based on truths, or more likely, partial truths. Propaganda is *not* necessarily based on blatant falsehoods as it largely was in Hitler's Third Reich. Unfortunately, many still think of the word in this way.

Take a look around you and I think you'll see that you're bombarded almost constantly with propaganda messages. Politicians, lobbyists, ad men, public relations practitioners— in fact, almost anyone who's trying to sell an idea, product or service—all are trying to win you over with "legitimate" propaganda tactics. So are your opponents at the negotiating table in most cases.

HOW TO USE FACTS AND FIGURES

Thus, in order to become a true power negotiator, you'll need to add a few propaganda tactics to your repertoire. One highly popular technique is to be able to use facts and figures authoritatively. Despite Disraeli's admonition about "liars, damned liars and statisticians," many are convinced by authoritatively-stated facts and figures.

The earlier example in which three different parties quoted different average prices for homes in Dallas is a case in point. Each had a different goal. One's was to convince a manufacturer that his city had *moderately* priced homes; another's was to impress a prospect with his city's level of affluence; and the other's was to convince his conservative investors that his community was a solid, middle-of-the-road economic entity.

Propaganda? Yes, without a doubt. But the point is: all of the "average" prices quoted *could* have been correct, and probably were. It all depends on how you interpret the word *average*. This is the essence of power negotiating through propaganda: knowing how and when to use facts and figures, and other information, to *your* advantage.

Qualifying That Average

None of the Dallas negotiators was really misrepresenting his case, since an average can be one of three things.

First, there is the arithmetic *mean*. This average is gained by taking the total price of all homes sold and dividing this figure by the total number of homes sold. Next there's the *median*. This average is the midpoint; half the homes sold were above this price, half were below it. And finally, there's the *mode*, the price at which most homes in the group were sold.

All these—mean, median and mode—are averages, strictly speaking. The successful power negotiator (who more often than not is an adroit propagandist) realizes this fact and selects the average that best suits his or her particular needs and interests during the transaction.

What Is an Average Salary?

For example, a spokesman for the employees of a factory might claim that the average pay for his fellow workers is $13,000 a year. Since he's obviously trying to convince the public that workers are grossly underpaid, he selects the mode salary average. This, you'll recall, is the salary that a majority of employees receive.

On the other hand, a top management spokesman for the same company would likely claim that the average pay for employees was closer to $18,000. This would probably be a mean average; that is, the total salaries divided by the total number employees.

Actually, the typical employee would likely earn closer to the $13,000 figure, since the mean average would be boosted considerably by the Chairman of the Board and others in the executive hierarchy.

Still, both negotiators were "correct." They were simply using the average that best suited their purpose. One wanted the public to feel employees were underpaid; the other wanted the public to think its employees were very well paid.

Qualifying Is Necessary

In this case, both negotiators were highly skilled and knew how to use statistical information to their advantage. In many other instances, less skilled negotiators would not have been as knowledgeable.

The reason, I think, is because the public is generally unaware of the fact that an *unqualified* average can be meaningless. One prime reason for this is that the media often use the term rather loosely, and often incorrectly. They make reference to the average family income, average cost of living, average cost of housing, ad infinitum, without saying whether the average is a mean, median or mode. Even when the distinction is made, it frequently has little literal meaning to the "average" reader, who is not steeped in statistics.

Thus, as a power negotiator, you should be able to use averages to your advantage against unskilled negotiators. And conversely, you need to be able to defend yourself against unqualified averages when used by skilled negotiators against you.

Figures Can Be Confusing

But averages aren't the only "funny" figures you'll run into. Numbers in general can be quite confusing, and often misleading. For example, I often get confused when I go to the super market. Do I buy the 36-ounce bag of sugar for $1.47, or the 42-ounce bag for $1.83? If potatoes are 47 cents a pound, how much do I pay for 2¾ pounds? These numbers confuse me, and without the benefit of a hand calculator, quite frankly I wouldn't know how to negotiate this kind of deal.

Now, if little figures like this are frequently confusing to the general public, how about the more complex facts and figures? I submit that it is mind boggling to deal with such enigmatic issues as the cost of living index, national unemployment, Dow-Jones fluctuations and the like. And even if you understand double-entry bookkeeping, who among us can actually figure out corporate financial statements?

Developing a Defense

Without a doubt, you can improve your position as a power negotiator by learning to use statistical information to your advantage. On the other hand, it's equally important to learn how to "defend" yourself against negotiators who try to dazzle *you* with a statistical barrage.

For example, let's take a quick look at how you might use statistics—first as a banker or investor, and then as a borrower—in negotiating a loan.

Quoting Interest Rates

Assume your banker had tentatively agreed to giving you a 11¼ percent loan, but when it came time to close the loan, he said, "I'm sorry, but we weren't able to get you that 11¼ percent loan after all. The Fed went up on its rate last week, so the best we can do for you is 11¾ percent. But after all, that'll amount to just a few extra dollars a month." Sounds logical, doesn't it? Well, actually that "insignificant" ½ percent additional interest will add up to thousands of dollars on a $50,000 loan over a 30-year period.

So how should you, as a power negotiator, respond to this propaganda tactic? Perhaps something like this: "Look, Mr. Banker, I can appreciate the fact that the cost of money has gone up. But look, you *did* agree to a 11¼ percent loan. Where I come from, a deal's a deal, and I'm sure you like to do business this way, too. Incidentally, tell me, just how much would that ½ percent in interest add up to over 30 years?"

Now you've put the ball back in his court. You just might have intimidated him into keeping his word. And in any case, you have forced him to *show* you that the additional ½ percent interest will be quite costly over the long haul.

A similar incident occurred when an astute union

negotiator asked for, among other things, a "mere five minutes more" in break time. The company spokesman readily agreed, not realizing that the additional five minutes, spread over the entire work force, would add up to a significant loss of production time.

REDUCING TO THE RIDICULOUS

Making facts and figures more acceptable is a technique that has been mastered by most successful salespeople. One such tactic is called "reducing to the ridiculous."

Let's assume, for example, that as a real estate salesman, you have a buyer who is willing to pay $60,000 for a property and no more. The seller, however, won't take a penny less than $62,000.

True, $2,000 is a lot of money, enough in this case to keep the buyer from closing the deal. Thus, the astute real estate dealer talks *not* in terms of $2,000, but of a smaller, more manageable sum. He responds:

$2,000 to 60 cents

"Mr. Buyer, I realize that $2,000 seems like a lot of money, and it is. But let me explain it this way. As a rule of thumb in real estate, each additional $1,000 on the loan amounts to about $9 a month in house payment. This means $2,000 would increase your house payment by only $18 a month. Now, that $18, broken down into a daily cost, comes to only 60 cents a day. In other words, for the cost of only a package of cigarettes a day, you can move right into a home that you've admitted suits your every need. Don't you agree?"

Frequently, the buyer *will* agree. It's easier to take when a seemingly large sum of money is reduced to the ridiculous.

Making Your Numbers Precise

It's important that the information you use to propagandize your cause be valid and if possible, of substance. But *how* you present this information can be equally important.

For example, the trend in most negotiations is to "round off" numbers. A negotiator might say, "The average salary of the typical American family is $13,000," or "The average American consumes about 100 pounds of beef annually," or "The tolerance on our machine is about 1/100th of an inch."

Convincing? Perhaps. But I suggest you can add credibility to your comments by doing just the opposite. Instead of making statements that are general, make them as *specific* as possible. For instance: "The average salary of the typical American family is $12,679.53," or "The average American consumes 98.73 pounds of beef annually," or "The tolerance on our machine is .0001117 of an inch."

Quoting from "Reliable" Sources

Why is the detailed figure more likely to be more convincing? Because it *sounds* more authentic. "That figure *must* be right," your opposition is likely to think. "Surely he couldn't have just dreamed it up."

There's still another way to add credibility to the facts and figures you quote in your negotiation. You can quote *liberally* from generally reliable and prestigious sources.

Why does this tactic frequently work quite well? Mainly because we're conditioned to such quotations. If you read a daily newspaper, for example, you have no doubt discovered that much of the information is attributed to "reliable," "unimpeachable," or "authoritative" sources. The more prestigious your source, the greater your credibility is likely to be.

The "Evidence" Technique in Action

Here's where the evidence technique I mentioned earlier can come in handy. As a Realtor, you'll recall, I sometimes suggested to reluctant sellers that I could probably get them eight or nine percent more for their property than they could get selling it themselves.

The reason, I explained, was my knowledge of real estate and heavy negotiating experience in this area. I was also quick to point out that I was more likely to be able to do this on larger, custom-built homes, where price is more difficult to establish.

Did sellers typically believe such a boast? I think not. The idea just didn't sound reasonable. That's why I eventually got two pieces of evidence to back up my claim. One was an article from the highly regarded *Washington Post*, quoting the findings of a Realtor-engineer-columnist, who came to this conclusion after conducting a 10-year survey on the subject.

The other was from the *Reader's Digest*. It was written by a much-travelled citizen who had moved across the country scores of times. He had sold his own home on several occasions and used a Realtor on several others. His conclusion: you can usually save money by going through an experienced real estate person, even after paying the commission. In many cases, showing sellers copies of these articles made my negotiation easier—and more successful.

Negotiating a Training Program

Another brief story illustrates the point. In this case, I was trying to sell a training program on "Conducting Profitable Business Meetings" to a certain company. I outlined the program in our initial negotiation, but got nowhere. The people just didn't seem to be impressed.

Sensing that I hadn't made an overwhelming impression, I arranged another meeting. In this one, I displayed a cassette program and workbook on which the training program was to be based. The program was published by American Management Association, and I feel certain this was a major factor in their decision to buy.

No question about it. The company representatives were more impressed with AMA than they were with me. But the punch line is, *I* wrote the AMA program!

Matching Publications

Since that time, I've learned to play this game of *quotesmanship* much better, I think. In the planning stage of any upcoming negotiation these days, I search out relevant articles from prestigious publications and use them as part of my presentation.

I usually try to "fit" the publication with the negotiation at hand. For example, if the negotiation is about, say, a management-development program for a corporation, I try to find recent and relevant articles from such publications as *The Wall Street Journal, Fortune, Harvard Business Review*, and the like. These publications carry considerable clout with most corporate types.

If my opponent is a sports buff, I switch to publications like *Sports Illustrated* or *The Sporting News*. If the negotiation concerns technical issues, I seek information from leading trade publications in that particular industry or profession. And so forth.

FINDING FACTS IN A HURRY

Before you can *present* facts effectively, you obviously have to "find" them. Knowing *when* and *where* to get information—usually in a hurry—is a prerequisite to success in power negotiating.

Quite often, if you can swing it, the most reliable way to get information is directly from the source. I've known negotiators who have greatly improved their negotiating posture because of information gained directly from the president of a major corporation, a college president, a well-known sports star and a best-selling author.

It can be very impressive to let your opponent know that you got your information "straight from the horse's mouth."

Bidding for a Franchise

For instance, a Dallas entrepreneur became quite interested in a self-improvement course being franchised across the country by a New York organization. The course was based on a best-selling book, which ranked behind only *How to Win Friends and Influence People* in all-time popularity.

The program looked promising. However, the Dallas man felt the initial fee for the Southwest territory was exorbitant. He objected, too, to the attendance guarantee the franchisor was demanding.

Though the businessman was highly impressed with the book and the few secondhand reports he had received about the course (none from anyone who had actually run the course), he was hesitant to make a large financial commitment without further information.

It was at this point that the businessman called the author of the book directly. The author gladly furnished him with the names of a half dozen franchises which had actually been in operation for a short period of time. This was information that had *not* been volunteered by the franchise salesman.

Investigation Pays Off

What did the experienced franchisees think of the course? Consensus was that it had great potential, but needed considerable revising before it could be called a truly dynamic, turnkey program.

The Dallas businessman confronted the franchisor with the information at the final negotiation. As a result, he was able to purchase the franchise for a fraction of the original asking price. And he was able to insist that the franchisor drop his original attendance demands. Obviously, he minimized his risk considerably.

Gathering information directly either by mail or phone frequently helps in several important ways. It obviously makes your inputs more timely, and often more reliable. It can yield little-known or previously unpublished facts that can sometimes make the difference in your negotiation.

How to Use a Library

Again, direct contact is usually the fastest and often the most effective way to gain facts that can give you negotiating leverage. Obviously, however, it's frequently neither practical nor expedient to go straight to the source. Many—perhaps *most*—of your negotiations will require your probing for the facts from a variety of sources.

If you're pressed for time, one of your very best sources of information might well be the "Information Center" of a metropolitan library.

Manager Preps for Negotiation

Let's assume, for example, that you're the marketing manager for a large computer company. In the main, your company develops programs to handle accounting problems for a variety of small to medium-sized businesses.

Your job is to select a promising market for your system, then to sell this idea to a hard-nosed management. You are currently making up such a program for the hotel-motel industry, and the deadline for negotiating your deal with management is tomorrow afternoon.

Your research has been fairly comprehensive. Still, you discover at the last minute that you need several vital facts: How many hotels are there in the 100-to-300 room range which you have belatedly decided to target in on? What is the financial condition of a certain chain of motels which you consider to be a prime prospect? What credence can you give to rumors of a top-management shake-up in still another hotel chain? And finally, what have been the stock market fluctuations of still another hotel chain?

Finding Facts in a Hurry

Getting the answers to these questions is vital to your impending negotiation. But there just doesn't appear to be enough time for further research.

The solution? Contact the information center of your metropolitan library. You will probably get your answers within minutes.

For example, the Dallas library's center has a 10-person staff which is geared to answering such queries as the ones just mentioned. And the number of queries has increased steadily since the center's inception in 1974. The center is a veritable gold mine of facts for the business and professional person. And the only tool needed to work this mine is just an arm's reach away—your telephone.

Annual Reports Available

Take the question about the financial condition of a certain hotel chain. The center has annual reports on microfilm for practically all of America's major corporations. In addition, actual copies of annual reports for thousands of firms are available if you want to drop by and inspect them in detail.

"Marketing inquiries are not uncommon," a library spokesman said. "We get scores of calls daily from marketing people who want to know how many cases of a brand food or drink have sold in a certain region lately. They also want to know things like, "What is the projected growth pattern for New Mexico? What are the buying habits of people for a certain toothpaste in New Orleans? What are the sales figures for a certain company in the final quarter of last year? We handle most of these calls rather expeditiously."

"However," he added, "we do get stumped on occasion. One caller wanted to know how many baby bottles were sold in Corpus Christi, Texas, during the previous year. Frankly, we didn't have an answer. But eventually, we came up with an educated guess, which is really all the caller wanted anyway."

Searching Journals and Papers

The educated guess came from perusing one of well over 1,000 trade journals the library keeps on file. These journals represent virtually every business, trade, and profession.

And if you need to know where some of the nation's leading newspapers and magazines stand editorially on certain issues—an important point in some negotiations—the center in Dallas can probably help.

"We stand anywhere from two weeks, perhaps up to a month behind, on editorials and other excerpts from major newspapers like the *Los Angeles Times, Washington Post* and *Chicago Tribune*," the library spokesman said. "This is about as current a service as you can get anywhere."

Making a Firsthand Probe

Frequently, however, it takes more than a telephone call to get the in-depth information you'll need on some subjects. But the resources are available in most metropolitan libraries if you know how to use them.

For example, the president of a medium-sized manufacturer was put in the position of having to negotiate a four-day work week for his company. Previously, he had to negotiate the matter with his Board of Directors.

This case required several visits to the library to get the desired information. Finding up-to-the-minute facts about such "contemporary" subjects as this, on which relatively little has been written, is no easy chore. But it usually can be done if you know how and where to get the facts.

Guides Are Good Source

The president, after consulting with the librarian, first took a look at the *Reader's Guide to Periodical Literature*. Published twice monthly, the guide lists the contents of nearly 150 of the most popular current magazines, along with a few scholarly and scientific publications. It tells when and where articles are published, and on which page the article can be found.

In this case, the guide listed a number of interesting articles on the subject and at least one good book.

His research revealed this. Consensus is that the four-day week is alive and thriving, especially in small retail stores, hospitals, banks and police departments. "Big names" include a Samsonite plant in Murfreesboro, Tennessee; Armour's plant in Fairmount, Minnesota; and Method Life Insurance

Company's Computer Division. United Steelworkers Union had announced the four-day week as a goal. Overall, response seemed to be favorable.

This kind of "evidence" enabled the president to negotiate his cause from a position of relative strength.

Many Sources Available

There are a number of similar sources available. But perhaps the most current and comprehensive picture is afforded by the *New York Times Index*. It is on microfilm in most major libraries. Universally, the *Times* is regarded as a "newspaper of record." It prints virtually all events of national and international interest, and frequently runs full texts of items, including speeches, described only briefly in other newspapers and magazines. The *Times* has been carefully indexed since its inception in 1851.

The *Monthly Catalog of United States Government Publications*, issued by the Superintendent of Documents in Washington, D. C., is another outstanding source, as are other indexes on medical and technical subjects.

Center Has Limitations

Naturally, the staff at the center in Dallas, like library staffs elsewhere, will not engage in extensive research for you. But they will gladly offer guidance on where you can get information.

Questions about legal and medical terms are usually taboo for obvious reasons. And telephone queries that require special knowledge, such as a chemical formula, are transferred to the appropriate department.

Becoming your own researcher takes some time and effort. But it's an effort most power negotiators are willing to make.

Chapter 9

KNOWING WHEN TO BREAK OFF NEGOTIATIONS

While browsing around an antique shop, my wife and I spotted an old clock that was "made" for our Early American den. "How much?" we asked excitedly.

Sensing our enthusiasm, the owner seemed to hedge. "Well, I don't know," he said. "We just got that old clock in last week. I'll have to check it out. Offhand, though, I'd say it was worth at least $700."

"That's ridiculous," we countered. "There's no way that clock is worth anywhere *near* $700." We felt certain the owner was highballing us. Thus our strategy was to return the next day, offer $500, and if absolutely necessary, go as high as $600.

Goes Up, Not Down

But our plan backfired. "I'm sorry," the owner said after we had made our $500 offer, "but I've checked the clock out and it's more valuable than we at first thought. It's a real collector's item. I'll have to raise the price to $800. And believe me, it's a bargain at that."

Our surprise quickly turned to indignation. "Look," we said, "you quoted us a price of $700. Are you going to stick to your word or not?"

After showing appropriate "dismay" at having to sell his clock for such a low figure, the owner finally agreed to his original price of $700. Tired of hassling and now wanting the clock more than ever, we bought it at the owner's price.

COMMITMENT IS THE ANSWER

Were we disappointed? On the surface, yes. But secretly, we were *delighted* to pay the escalated price for the coveted clock. Why? Because we had mentally *committed* ourselves to owning it.

I think this is mainly why *escalation* works so well as a negotiating tactic. Once a person feels he not only needs but badly *wants* to buy, few things can stand in his way, including cost.

Recognizing this, you can frequently use escalation to wrest top dollar from an overly eager buyer.

However, the technique should be used with utmost discretion. Using it inopportunely can not only cause you to lose a sale, but the good will of a potential long-range customer. Used properly, the technique can help protect your interests in a negotiation.

Seller Escalates Price

For example, a home owner agreed to list his home for sale through a Realtor for $80,000. Two months later, a buyer agreed to buy the home at the full list price.

However, between the time the home was listed and sold, the discount points charged to the seller increased from one to five points. "Points," as mentioned earlier, are charged by the investor to make up the difference between what he could get on a real estate loan and some other form of investment.

One point equals one percent of the loan. So in this case,

the seller would have been forced to pay five points on a $70,000 loan—a hefty $3,500 above and beyond the sales commission and other regular closing costs.

As a result, the seller escalated the price of his home from $80,000 to $84,000 to cover these additional costs that he had not anticipated, and to net him what he wanted for the home in the first place.

How the Tactic Can Backfire

In this case, the seller and Realtor used escalation to protect their best interests. But I recall another case in which escalation was used inadvisedly and backfired on the Realtor.

In this instance, the seller had just sold his home through a Realtor. Unfortunately, there had not been good communication. The Realtor had told the seller at the time of listing that his total costs would include the commission, plus "routine closing costs." There was *no* mention of discount points.

Understandably, the seller was furious to learn from the title company attorney at closing that his costs would include $4,200 for commission, $3,400 for discount points and $450 for miscellaneous closing costs.

The seller threatened to back out of the transaction. And for a brief period, he did actually leave the title company. But in the end, he returned and closed the deal. Why? Again, because he had already made up his mind to sell. It is this type of mental commitment that causes the escalation technique to work so well—better, in many cases, than it should.

Tactic Questionable Here

There is some question in this case whether escalation was used wisely. Real estate people, like others who sell services, usually rely rather heavily on strong referrals from satisfied customers. This disgruntled seller would no doubt have criticized the Realtor for some time to come.

Probably the agent who handled the deal was a novice.

Most Realtors I know are completely candid in quoting *all* costs to buyers and sellers.

Still, escalation is a powerful technique, one every power negotiator needs in his arsenal.

HOW HITLER USED ESCALATION

There appears to be another reason escalation works well. It's because of the negotiating truism that if you can find out what the other person will submit to, you will know exactly how far you can go in dealing with that person. You have no doubt seen this principle at work in many marriages and business relationships. The idea can work just as effectively in international politics, as Adolph Hitler demonstrated.

Except for a flaw in character, Hitler might well have been considered the prototype of a power negotiator. He had a deep understanding of the nature of power, an extremely high aspiration level, and an uncanny ability to make accurate assumptions. And, as history shows, he was a master at using the escalation technique.

Hitler's negotiating prowess began to surface after World War I. First, he gained leadership of the Nazi Party, which was to eventually control Germany. Then, he swiftly— against prohibitive odds—became absolute dictator of Germany.

After proving himself a classic power negotiator within his own country, Hitler began to pit his negotiating skills against *world* powers, in effect, he escalated his area of influence. For starters, he launched compulsory military service, an act prohibited by the Versailles Treaty. Having tested his assumption and having discovered that he could violate the treaty virtually at will, Hitler escalated his rebuilding effort. He started by strengthening the Luftwaffe, the vaunted German Air Force, and the German Army.

Juggernaut Is Built

After "negotiating" an Army and Air Force, Hitler continued to up the ante. He next negotiated a pact with Great

Britain (also against the Versailles Treaty) to build a Navy one third the size of England's. This included deadly U-boats.

Having built a military juggernaut, Hitler then began to escalate his demands on European real estate at an unprecedented rate.

First, he occupied the Rhineland, which was set up as a buffer between France and Germany after World War I. France complained to the League of Nations but took no action. Shortly thereafter, Hitler scored another negotiating coup by taking over his native Austria. Both England and France complained vehmently—but took no action!

Takeovers Continue

Czechoslavakia was next in line, despite France's commitment to protecting the Czechs against invasion and a two-to-one troop advantage by France and Czechoslovakia. England protested loudly and sent its Prime Minister, Neville Chamberlain, to negotiate with Hitler. Chamberlain returned home with his famous peace-for-our-time pronouncement. But shortly thereafter, Hitler again escalated his demands and this time took over Czechoslavakia against only token resistance.

Hitler then negotiated a nonaggression pact with Russia, enabling him to later invade Poland without fear of intervention by the Soviet. He had again correctly assumed that France and England would not interfere. Finally, Hitler had escalated one step too many, and the Allies went to war against him. But the escalation tactic had netted him enormous gains with only minor resistance.

Discretion Is Urged

Again, the very nature of the escalation technique dictates that it be used with discretion in your social and business affairs. Remember, negotiation is a two-way street in which both parties need to gain *something* from the transaction. Unwarranted escalation can only cause the other party to lose face, putting a damper on future harmonious relations with that party.

As a power negotiator, you'll need to master the technique of escalation so that you can use it at the proper moment. At the same time, you'll need to develop suitable defenses when others use the tactic *against* you.

What If the Bluff Fails?

One defense is simply to call the other person's bluff. For example, what would have happened if the Allies had called Hitler's hand when he started illegally to rebuild his war machine? If France had resisted when he took over the Rhineland? If France and England had prevented his takeover of Czechoslavakia? Chances are, with military supremacy in their favor, then they would have prevented World War II.

Calling the other party's bluff can, of course, be risky. It entails your being willing to swing into action if the other party persists in using unwarranted escalation tactics.

Get Agreement in Writing

Another defense against escalation is to *get it in writing*. If you're selling your home, for example, have it put in your listing agreement that you won't pay above the prevailing discount points. If you're buying, get locked in on the current interest rate.

What if the real estate person refuses to have these items written into the contract? Find yourself another agent. It's a competitive business and there will always be an agent who will put it in the contract if you press the issue strongly enough. Simply make it a condition of doing business.

Other Side of the Coin: De-Escalation

De-escalation can work as well. Assume, for example, that a contractor offers to build a room onto your home for $8,000, then later escalates the price to $9,000.

"Sorry," you reply, "but I've taken another look at the budget, and I overestimated. All I can afford is $7,500 tops."

There's a danger, of course, that the contractor will back out. But chances are, the contractor will get the price down to $7,500 by eliminating a few frills or cutting a corner here or there. Like the buyer who has mentally committed himself to buying, the seller has mentally made the sale. It's amazing how ingenious sellers can get when faced with the possibility of losing business they felt they already had in the bag.

SURPRISE CAN BE EFFECTIVE

Escalation, by its very nature, most often carries with it the element of *surprise*, which in itself can be a formidable negotiating tactic. Surprise can take many shapes and forms, such as changing price, location, issues, negotiators, or other agreed-upon practices.

I can think of a couple of situations in which surprising the other party with a change of one or more of these factors enabled the power negotiator to achieve his goals.

In one case, the advertising manager of a new division of a computer company was negotiating a new contract with a well-known advertising agency. Since the computer company was incurring heavy start-up costs, the advertising manager had instructions to keep costs as low as possible.

How the Ad Manager Gets Price Down

The ad manager heard proposals from several agencies. He was particularly pleased with the imaginative approach taken by XYZ Agency. Unfortunately, XYZ's cost estimate was quite a bit higher than those submitted by the others. Trying hard to conceal his enthusiasm for XYZ's campaign strategy, the ad manager arranged a special meeting with XYZ's top brass. Mission: to lower the cost of the agency's proposal.

The meeting was scheduled to last two hours, but ran all day and well into the evening. Agency representatives spent hours cost-justifying its innovative campaign strategy aimed at putting the computer company on the map.

Finally, the agency agreed to reduce its costs by five percent. What the agency did not know was that the ad manager had decided he could not possibly sell the program to his top management without a 10 percent reduction.

Company Sends in "Sub"

"Okay," the ad manager said, "it's looking a little better. We still can't go at that figure, but let's sleep on it and hit it again bright and early in the morning." The beleaguered ad agency executives could do little but agree.

Everyone showed up for the meeting bright and early the next morning. Everyone, that is, except the ad manager. He had been called out of town on "pressing company business." The computer company's public relations manager had taken his place.

Agency representatives had understandably expected to wrap this session up in an hour or so. However, the public relations manager wanted to hear all the details of the campaign, especially the cost-justification, over and over again. In the end, the harried agency representatives agreed to a 10 percent cost reduction, eliminating only minor parts of its projected campaign.

How Switch Affects Opponent

The surprise in this negotiation was, of course, the new negotiator. And what did this premeditated action cause? Well, for starters it caused the ad agency people to *resell* their program. They had to negotiate with an entirely different person (one who, incidentally, had only limited authority), and in the course of the negotiation, answer a new round of objections. In the aggregate, these factors wore down the agency negotiators and ultimately forced them to meet the computer company's terms.

In addition, the public relations director was finally able

to swing the deal in his favor through a negotiating tactic that is as old as time itself: *bribery*. He strongly *implied* that if the ad agency would go along at his price, it would be in a "strong position" to compete for some of the computer company's corporate business the next year.

Negotiating a Plane Price

The other negotiation in which surprise played a key role was between a government investigation team and a leading aerospace firm. The investigators were trying to arrive at a fixed price for a soon-to-be-built fighter plane.

Since the airplane was being built for both the Air Force and the Navy, it was supposed to have a high degree of what the government called *commonality*—that is, a high percentage of aircraft parts and systems would be common to both airplanes. A high degree of commonality would theoretically save the government a great deal of money.

When government investigators tried to put a firm price on the aircraft they ran into all sorts of "surprises" from the aerospace firm's negotiating team of engineers, technical experts and management people.

The aerospace team fouled up the agenda time after time with lengthy digressions into technical issues. For example, the team pointed out that certain parts of the plane were to be built from titanium and boron composites, two new lightweight materials that had unknown qualities. Both would entail many hours of additional research before their reliability could be checked out. Did the government want this experimentation to continue? If so, precisely how much time and effort should be spent on such a program? And how would all this affect price?

Issue Becomes Clouded

Then, too, there were sophisticated new avionics systems to be built into the plane. These systems would advance the state of the art. The net result was that the negotiation bogged down in extraneous technical issues. Somehow the idea of putting a fixed price on the plane (and pinning the aerospace firm down) got lost in the shuffle.

The advantage in this instance again went to the team that invoked the element of *surprise* in the negotiation; they used it as a specific technique to get their point across.

Changing negotiators, introducing new facts, modifying issues, changing your *own* position—these are but some of the surprise tactics that can be used successfully on occasion by the power negotiator.

Offense Is Best Defense

What is the best *defense* against the surprise tactic? Probably it is to *counterattack*! If the opposition brings in a new negotiator, bring in one of your own, or refuse to deal with the new person. If the other party switches issues, call his hand. Make him stick to the agenda. Whatever the opposition does, in other words, try to go it one better.

While surprise can be a powerful negotiating tactic (Remember Pearl Harbor! Or more appropriately, remember how mad it made America and how quickly and lethally the country responded to the challenge.), it could be a mistake to surprise your opponent too much or too often.

BLUFFING TAKES SEVERAL FORMS

Bluffing can be an effective power negotiating technique in some cases, and it comes in various forms, such as: delivering an *ultimatum* to your opponent; making a *last and final offer*; or threatening to *withdraw* from a negotiation.

All these tactics *can* be effective. But all carry the risk of the opposition "calling your hand," whereupon you must carry out your bluff or back down and lose face—and negotiating leverage.

Negotiating in these areas is not unlike playing poker. You have to know when to hold, when to fold, and when to bluff. A bluffing technique brings to bear all of your negotiating powers. To a heightened degree, you need to know how to make and test *assumptions*. Obviously a seasoned power negotiator is going to assume that his opponent has neither the will nor the inclination to call his hand.

Dealer Assumes Correctly

The antique dealer who sold us the old clock, you'll recall, assumed correctly that we wanted the antique very badly. Badly enough, perhaps, to pay more than the list price.

Based on this assumption, he first escalated his price to what, in retrospect, was an unreasonable level, then "came down" to this price again after escalating to a totally unrealistic figure. There's little doubt in my mind that his "last and final offer" was *firm* because he had recognized our real desire to own the clock. His assumption was valid.

Kennedy Threatens Cuba

Bluffing in one form or another is carried on at the highest level of international relations. In such cases, the stakes are understandably much higher.

For example, the late President John F. Kennedy ordered Russia to remove its anti-ballistic missile system from Cuba in 1962, then boldly ordered a naval blockade thrown up around that country to prevent the arrival of additional Soviet arms support. His *ultimatum* was clear and unmistakable: get your missiles out of Cuba, or else!

Or else what? What, for example, if the Soviets had failed to remove the ICBMs in Cuba? What if they had attempted to run the blockade? Would the United States then have taken military action? Herein lies the potential danger in using a bluff or threat in any form. You must be prepared to pay the consequences—either that or lose face with the rest of the world. Providentially, Kennedy's assumption turned out to be a correct one.

This brand of diplomacy, called *brinksmanship*, was created by former Secretary of State John Foster Dulles. It implied massive retaliation if the opposition failed to heed a

United States ultimatum. It was quite effective for awhile. But the consequences of using such a strategy are, indeed, mind boggling.

Executive Gives Ultimatum

The ultimatum power game is played quite frequently in the business world. For example, an executive in a medium-sized manufacturing plant became dissatisfied with his plight. He had helped nurture the company through its growing pains and felt he was being passed over for promotion.

As a result, he tried a bluff. Although he had not received an offer of any kind, he informed his president that he had been approached by a competitor to fill a key spot similar to the one he now held. "If you want me to stay on," he said, "you'll have to give me more money and put me on your Board of Directors."

The bluff worked, primarily because the executive's company felt his particular expertise would give its competitor an edge in a highly specialized area. But as any good bluffer should, the executive had planned the steps he would take if the bluff failed, and was prepared to take them.

Koreans Use Withdrawal

Withdrawal from a negotiation can be another form of bluffing. North Korean negotiators used this and a variety of other power negotiating tactics at the Panmunjom Peace Talks. It seems they were either threatening to walk out—or actually walking out—almost continuously during these lengthy deliberations. They used these tactics with amazingly effective results, as we'll discuss more fully in a later chapter.

So what's the bottom line on using the several variations of the bluffing power negotiating technique? Perhaps to a degree, you can follow the same general rule of thumb you'd follow in a poker game. Go ahead and bluff if you feel your opponent will go for it. But be prepared to pay the price if someone calls your hand.

Chapter 10

GAINING A DOMINANT POSITION IN PERSONAL RELATIONS THROUGH POWER NEGOTIATING

A Dallas attorney I know possesses many of the attributes of a power negotiator. He is intelligent, perceptive and conscientious. Further, he usually becomes *totally* familiar with the issues before entering a negotiation.

Despite these virtues, he is generally *not* conceded to be a top-notch negotiator. Why? Mainly because he doesn't *look*, *act* or *talk* like one. In short, he does not communicate well.

COMMUNICATION AS THE KEY

Issues quite obviously become the pivotal point in almost any negotiation. But it is the way these issues are presented that often makes the difference between success and failure in negotiating.

Communication, as used in this sense, means several things: developing the *look* and *feel* of power; mastering a variety of proven verbal tactics (as well as an understanding of nonverbal communication); and finally, developing strong *active* listening habits. Mastering these basic communication skills, along with the issues involved in a transaction, can upgrade your status to that of power negotiator.

DEVELOPING THE LOOK AND FEEL OF POWER

All other things being equal, you'll recall, the negotiator who *expects* to win usually does. A high aspiration level is definitely one of the chief attributes of a power negotiator. This aspiration level usually relates to a negotiator's ability to understand and use *power*.

For example, in a negotiation between a corporal and a captain, or a vice president and a secretary, the power positions are quite clear. The corporal and the secretary usually negotiate with a relatively low expectation level (though there are ways for the "underdog" to gain a degree of parity, as we'll discuss in the following chapter).

In many, perhaps most of your daily negotiations, you'll be negotiating with "peers." So when no one is wearing "stripes," who then achieves "superiority?" By and large, it will be the person who has the higher expectation level and who understands the nature and use of power.

Dress Is an Indicator

How can you *tell* who has the higher power status? Perhaps more than anything else by the way the person looks and acts. How you dress is one strong indicator. A best-selling book points out that America is run by men and women who dress in a conservative, conventional way.

Extensive research, including a number of public tests, shows that people who dress this way tend to get preferential treatment in business affairs, including negotiations. Chances are good that in a negotiation between a well-dressed and a not-so-well-dressed negotiator, the former will gain leverage.

Tests show that dark blue and gray suits, with complementary shirts and ties, help appreciably in a higher-level transaction. The suit need not be expensive, but well-known brands such as Hickey-Freeman, Hart Schaffner & Marx, and Brooks Brothers can add authority at upper-level confabulations.

Experts say women who are now finding their way into upper-echelon professional and executive spots, must make a point of dressing with more *authority*. This clear feedback from top male executives is that a conservative, dark-colored skirted suit and blouse is the combination most likely to give a woman this kind of authority.

Good Health Can Help

Good health can also create an aura of power. I know a buyer from a big Dallas department store who does a great deal of his business during perhaps a half dozen trade shows during the year. Before each of these shows, he spends several days in Acapulco, drinking in sunshine. He then returns to the trade shows well rested and highly tanned. Technically, this healthy demeanor does little to make this person a more effective negotiator, but it makes him *feel* better about himself and thus tends to raise his all-important aspiration level.

A well-modulated voice, pleasing personality and good sense of humor are other traits which can add to a negotiator's power position. Other factors that add to power include sex, age, profession or business, and social background.

HOW TO USE POWERFUL VERBAL TACTICS

For the most part, however, your negotiating ability will be determined by your verbal and nonverbal skills, along with your ability to listen *actively*.

The Lord gave you two ears and one mouth. Obviously you're supposed to listen twice as much as you talk. This old saw will surely hold true in many negotiations. By all means, let your opposition do most of the talking.

The danger in *your* talking too much is obvious. The more you talk, the more likely you are to reveal information which might tip your hand—the last thing a good poker player or negotiator wants to do.

How Silence Pays Off

If you are not talking, two conditions exist. Either your opponent is talking or there is *silence*. Either situation *can* be healthy for you, depending on what you're trying to accomplish in your negotiation.

For example, most successful salespeople, who are negotiating every time they try to make a sale, recognize the devastating power of silence when used at the right place in the sales cycle.

One "right" time can be when the salesperson tries to get a commitment from a prospect. For example, the salesperson's closing question could be, "Well, Mr. Prospect, what do you think? This home meets all your requirements and it's well within your price range. Is there any reason we can't just go ahead and submit an offer today?"

First to Speak "Loses"

It's a tough question for the prospect, who must now make a decision. In many cases—perhaps most—the prospect will pause at some length before responding. After all, it takes time for most of us to make a big decision.

Such prolonged pauses are frequently interpreted as bad news by the inexperienced salesperson. When he fails to get a quick response, he keeps on selling, often talking himself right *out* of the sale.

But the more experienced salesperson generally follows the old sales axiom, "The first one who speaks, loses." Thus he waits and waits and waits, if necessary, even though the silence might seem interminable. He realizes that silence is a way of putting *legitimate* pressure on the other party. It forces him to take a course of action. Used properly, silence can add appreciably to your power position in a negotiation.

Getting Your Opponent to Talk

But where silence can, indeed, be golden when used at the right time in a negotiation, it is more often the ability to *get the other party to talk* which will gain you power at the negotiating table. And how do you get your opponent to give you the information you so badly need to gain leverage in the negotiation? By skillfully asking questions, direct and indirect.

An indirect, or open-end question is one that virtually demands that the other party give you an opinion rather than a "Yes" or "No" answer.

For example, let's take that same real estate broker we discovered a moment ago and put him in a situation that most salespeople run into routinely. The prospect's needs appear to be taken care of, but in the final analysis, the prospect says, "I want to think it over."

This objection, which frequently reflects a hidden, or unstated reason for not buying, brings the negotiation to an abrupt halt. But not necessarily for the skilled salesperson, who knows the power of a *direct* questioning technique.

How to Uncover an Objection

"Mr. Prospect," he'll respond, "I can appreciate your concern. It is a big decision. But since I'm here and my job is to answer any questions that might be in your mind, do you mind my asking a few questions?" (Without waiting for a response, he continues to ask direct questions.)

"Is there something about my company you're concerned with, or with me personally?"

"No, you seem quite competent, and I've checked your company out pretty thoroughly."

"You certainly appear to have the financial strength to handle the transaction. Any problems there I'm not familiar with?"

"No. None that I know of."

"How about the location?"

"Well, it's not bad at all. But it is a little farther from the city than we had planned on. Yes, I guess you could say we're concerned with the location all right."

When Direct Questions Help

Now the negotiation is reopened. Instead of having to deal with the enigmatic, "I want to think it over," the salesperson has a better chance of coping with a more specific objection. He has increased the probability of his effecting a successful negotiation.

This technique of asking a series of direct questions to arrive at a conclusion is often called the Socratic method of questioning, or interviewing. It is so called because Plato, in his dialogues, illustrated this method of Socrates, in which an opponent is led to draw his own conclusions.

It can be a most effective technique when your negotiation has reached an impasse and you are uncertain where your opposition stands on the issue, as in the case of a hidden objection.

Using Indirect Queries

It is the *indirect*, or open-end question which can be most effective for getting your opposite number to "open up." Assume, for example, that you're a personnel director charged with hiring a key executive for your company. Aside from certain technical knowledge, you are seeking someone with highly developed human relations skills—someone who can relate well to employees at all levels in the organization.

How can you tell in a brief interview whether the person has such skills? There is no way to tell for sure. But your chances of being able to make a sound judgment in this respect can be enhanced by the indirect method of questioning. Here's how such an interview might go:

Interview Is Sustained

Director: Well, Mr. Smith, according to your resume, you've certainly had some valuable experience. Do you mind my asking why you want to leave your present job?

Smith: Several reasons, really. For one thing I've reached the top of my pay bracket. There just doesn't seem to be any place to go. Then again, I feel I work best in an atmosphere where there's not so much politics.

Director: Politics?

Smith: Well, yes, there's a lot of it going on.

Director: How did you get personally involved in politics?

Smith: Well, it's a long story. But you see my job was to *sell* our systems, not to install them. I never could get that point across to our installation people that *their* job was to sell too. They just wouldn't go along.

Director: I see. Well, tell me, how do you feel about an equal employment policy?

Smith: I guess I've got some pretty strong views on that subject. For example, I like for. . . .

And so forth.

Counsellors Need This Skill

Smith then proceeded to tell, in some detail, how he felt about equal employment practices. The personnel director was able to get Smith's innermost thoughts on the subject because he knew how to ask significant indirect questions. Applicants for executive spots know how to skirt controversial issues rather adroitly. It takes a skilled negotiator (interviewer in this case) to draw out the real facts.

People who counsel others (and bear in mind that counselling is a continual negotiation) need to become highly adept at indirect interviewing, which again is based essentially on indirect questions.

The technique is really quite simple. You ask indirect questions, which compel the other party to give opinions rather than short, factual answers. You can keep the other party talking by occasionally injecting timely phrases such as, "I see," "You don't mean it," or simply, "Oh?" These phrases, in effect, say "I'm interested. Tell me more." And they usually do.

How to Answer a Question

Answering a question with a question is still another negotiating tactic aimed at keeping the other party talking, thus helping you control the interview. Listen in, for example, as a skilled real estate negotiator handles a telephone negotiation over an ad his company has run in the paper.

"What is the price of that home?"

"It's $75,000. Is that the price range you had in mind?"

"I suppose. How many square feet?"

"About 24,000. Would this suit your needs?"

"Sounds all right. What part of town is it in?"

"It's located in the Southwest. Is this the section you wanted?"

"Not really. My wife wants something in the West Side."

"I see. Well, we have many similar properties in that section of town. I'll be more than happy to arrange some showings for you . . ."

Questions Lead to Control

Who is controlling the interview? The salesman. And why? Because he is answering virtually every question with a question. In the process, he is qualifying his prospect and paving the way for a successful negotiation—a sale! With each question, he is removing a potential barrier to the sale.

This technique, like the others, must be used at the

appropriate time. An indiscreet or poorly timed question-to-a-question can be an impertinence. For example, there was the new salesman who had just learned the technique and practiced using it every time he could at home. One day his wife said, "Dear, why is it that here lately every time I ask a question, you ask a question?" He responded, "Yes, dear, why do you ask?"

CONTROLLED ANGER HAS A ROLE

One of the basic principles of effective negotiating is to maintain your cool. When you lose your temper, you're saying in effect that you're rattled; emotion has overruled logic. You are then vulnerable to tactics an opponent might use on you.

But controlled anger is another matter. In certain situations, it can be an effective verbal negotiating tactic.

"I use the technique on rare occasions," said Bob Ward, a veteran computer salesman, "but usually only as a last resort. Only after I've carefully qualified my prospect, taken considerable time to cost-justify the system, and written a proposal for him—and he *still* hasn't bought!

Only at this late stage does Ward show disappointment and mild—but very *controlled*—anger at the prospect for having "led him on." "Mr. Prospect," he'll remonstrate, "I think I'm entitled to some kind of explanation. We've spent a great deal of time together on this matter, and our system *does* seem to suit your needs perfectly. Is there anything that I've done personally to dissatisfy you?"

Ward not only uses the technique sparingly (for obvious reasons) but with utmost discretion. "You have to second-guess how your prospect is likely to take it," he said. "Used on some people, the tactic would get you thrown out on the spot."

Tossing a Rare Tantrum

If controlled anger is a negotiating technique to be used sparingly, *un*controlled anger is a tactic that should be used even less often. If used properly, however, on rare occasions, the tactic can be effective.

For example, how does a mother negotiate with a child who throws a tantrum? How does a salesperson handle a highly irrational client? How did foreign diplomats deal with Adolph Hitler's hysterical harangues? How does a subordinate deal with a highly irascible boss?

In each instance, I think you'll agree, the person who displayed bad temper was handled with kid gloves. The tendency in such situations is to make concessions and allowances you would not otherwise have made.

The point is, it is extremely difficult to negotiate with someone who will not listen to reason. The atmosphere becomes charged and emotion takes over. A wife probably gets more concessions from her husband during a crying spree than at any other time.

When "Dumb" Is "Smart"

Don't discount the *power of irrationality*. Sometimes it works far better than it should. But it *does* work. How do you defense against irrational behavior? Perhaps the best rule of thumb might be: simply don't put up with it. Once a spoiled child sees that his temper tantrum works, he'll escalate this behavior. And so, in all likelihood, will your irrational opponent.

Most of the time, you'll want to be a smart negotiator, but sometimes it's smart to be dumb. Have you ever tried to negotiate with someone who can't or won't understand the issues? It can be an exasperating experience, one that can ultimately force you to make concessions you wouldn't have made otherwise.

EXTRAPOLATION AT WORK

Extrapolation is a subtle negotiating tactic which aims at getting the other party to draw his own conclusion.

For example, a Fort Worth entrepreneur was attempting to franchise a business service he had operated successfully in the Dallas-Fort Worth area. He was entertaining a prospective franchise buyer from Chicago, who had come down to take a firsthand look at the operation.

The entrepreneur entertained the visitor at his palatial home. Impressed with what he saw, the visitor asked, "Mr. Smith, do you really think I could make it big with this type of operation?" The entrepreneur replied, "Let me put it this way. I own this home and several other properties. Last year, my various holdings grossed over $35 million, and I'm thinking about putting my franchise in at least two foreign countries."

Lets Opponent Draw Conclusion

What would you have concluded? Probably the same as the prospective franchisee, who felt certain the operation was going to make him rich.

From the facts given him (which might or might not have had a direct bearing on his ability to make money in a single franchise), the prospect drew his *own* conclusion—and this is the beauty of the technique. An opponent is much more likely to be convinced by his own opinion than someone else's. It matters not if the conclusion drawn was logical.

Salespeople usually love the technique because they realize that a prospect will staunchly defend a conclusion he draws himself. Try it the next time you get put in the position of having to give an answer which might "incriminate" you. Give your opponent the facts—usually *selected* facts which will tend to evoke a favorable response—and let him come to his own conclusion. This is almost certain to make him a believer.

USING NONVERBAL LANGUAGE TO GAIN ADVANTAGE

It would be remiss to discuss communication without mentioning the nonverbal aspect, commonly called body language. Make no mistake, our gestures and facial expressions can say as much as our words, and sometimes belie them.

Remember Bucky Woy, the flamboyant sports agent? Like most successful negotiators, he is highly sensitive to non-verbal feedback. In virtually every negotiation, he looks for some telltale sign which will tell him where he stands in the transaction.

"Many people will send a message of some kind," Woy said. "For instance, there's one party who literally seems to gasp for air when he's about ready to sign a big contract. I take this as my cue to hand him a pen and a contract."

"Another party 'tells' me he's about ready to close when he starts stuttering. "It's almost a sure-fire sign, since he's an otherwise highly articulate person."

Bill Lawrence Spots "Signs"

Bill Lawrence, a successful Oklahoma City Realtor, looks for "generalized" nonverbal signs. "Over the years," he said, "I have noticed that when a prospect sitting across the desk from you is ready to sign, he will almost invariably edge forward in his seat a bit. This tells me he's ready to close. So when he leans forward, I put a pen and sales contract in front of him. Sometimes, naturally, I get fooled, but not too often."

Lawrence, like most Realtors, also looks for "approving" or "disapproving" glances between couples when they're looking at property. "Buying is usually an emotional experience," he said. "This is why a *look* sometimes tells me more than words."

Reading Gestures Is Difficult

Body language experts claim that a sort of "universal" interpretation can be placed on certain movements. For example, a furrowed brow or raised eyebrow usually reflects doubt or concern. Slapping one's forehead shows forgetfulness. Scratching your nose shows doubt or puzzlement, while stroking your chin indicates a pensive mood. On the other hand, crossing your arms or legs shows resentment or opposition.

In reality, it is difficult, if not impossible, to let each gesture stand by itself. It becomes significant only when combined with the personalities of the individuals involved, the situation at hand, and the overall context. Only then can you get the real "message."

Besides, body language has become such a widely discussed subject these days that everybody is interpreting everybody else's movements. Thus some smart negotiators have learned not only to *mask* their real feelings, but to actually send out *false messages* which might throw the less knowledgeable negotiator off track.

Staking Out a "Territory"

Body language stems from serious studies by scholars done mostly on the living habits of animals. These studies reveal that most members of the animal kingdom stake out territories for their brood, then defend this area to the hilt. This innate desire to protect their selected area is called *territorial imperative*.

Scholars have concluded that humans also have a private air space, or comfort zone, invasion of which makes us uncomfortable and in some cases, hostile. This is an important fact to remember in negotiation, and one we'll discuss more fully later, along with how seating and furniture arrangement, among other factors, can affect more formal negotiations.

For now, suffice it to say that the generally acceptable distance between negotiators is normally from 24 to 36 inches. Anything closer than this is likely to be considered an invasion of one's privacy.

Using Postural Echo

The idea, where possible, is to use this principle to your advantage. One possible way to do this is through what is popularly called *postural echo*, wherein you subtly adapt the posture of your opponent.

For example, if your opponent crosses his knees, you cross yours. If he rests his chin in his hand, do likewise. If he finally sits back in his chair and crosses his arms, follow suit. All your imitative gestures should, quite obviously, be done subtly and with good timing. Otherwise, your opponent will think you are mimicking him. Executed properly, however, postural echo can help you establish rapport and empathy with your opponent. Why? Probably because imitation still happens to be one of the highest forms of flattery.

GAINING ADVANTAGE THROUGH ACTIVE LISTENING

"Is my hair as fine as flaxen?"
"Yep."
"Are my eyes bright as stars?"
"Yep."
"And are my lips as soft as rose petals?"
"Yep."
"Oh, Johnny, you're the most wonderful conversationalist."

Sound farfetched? Well, it isn't. Most of us feel that anyone who will listen attentively to our verbal volleys is not only astute, but probably very articulate. I feel reasonably certain that many fail to reach their full potential as negotiators because of their inability to fully understand and practice the active listening process.

The Nature of Listening

In the past few decades, educators have come up with several important conclusions about the listening process. They are:

● On routine information, you typically listen about four times faster than the other person talks.

● You retain only a relatively small percentage of what you hear—perhaps 25 percent in most cases.

● Your span of concentration is usually quite short. Trying to mentally stick to one subject for a full 30 seconds is a problem for most.

Indeed, listening is a complex process, and the negotiator who learns to listen actively will add appreciably to his or her negotiating powers. In the main, *active* listening entails your using more fully the mental time you have on your hands. How? Here are a few recommendations from successful power negotiators:

Signs of Active Listening

Think ahead. Use the "spare" mental time you usually have to second-guess your negotiating partner. Where is he heading in the discussion? What point is he trying to make? How will I react if he goes this way? That way? You'll keep yourself mentally active and your opponent "conversationally honest."

Listen critically. We're constantly bombarded with propaganda messages, including those from our opponents, during negotiations. Which facts and premises do you accept? Why? Which are you going to reject? Why?

Such analysis will keep your mental motor humming and at the same time help you make a sound assessment of your opponent's position. It will give you some live data for your rebuttal.

Listen for ideas as well as facts. Your opponent's facts are usually important only as they relate to main issues. One expert distinguishes between the two by drawing a line vertically down a sheet of paper and marking "ideas" on one side and "facts" on the other. He tries to correlate the two sides when the speaker has finished. In so doing, he determines the real "score."

Listen objectively. Try not to let your opponent's personality, however pleasant or abrasive, affect your analysis of his ideas. One of the most common listening faults is to tune people out because of appearance, dress or manner.

Question skillfully. Basically, the two main types of questions are *direct* and *indirect*. The latter, you'll recall, can be highly effective in sustaining a conversation and keeping the other party talking. Remember, the more the other person talks, the more you'll find out about his position on the issues—and the less inclined you'll be to stick your foot in your own mouth.

Top salespeople in most organizations might or might not be "glib talkers," but almost without exception, according to the president of one of the leading sales forces in the country, they're "glib listeners." I suspect the same idea holds true for just about every phase of power negotiating. The best negotiators are probably the best listeners.

Chapter 11

USING POWER NEGOTIATION WHEN YOU'RE THE UNDERDOG

At one time or another, you'll be the underdog in your negotiations. Your opponent will be favored to "win"—and often will—because of a superior power base, or expertise, or for other reasons.

But as you become a seasoned power negotiator, you'll learn to minimize your favored opponent's advantage, and in some cases, nullify it altogether. By using proven power negotiation tactics, you can compensate in varying degrees for your lack of leverage in such situations.

Some of the most capable underdogs I've seen in action are those who have learned to act with supreme confidence, even against seemingly overwhelming odds, and those who have developed a high degree of competence (that is, become somewhat of an expert) in a given area.

FRAN HUDSON GETS AWARD

Take Fran Hudson, for instance. She is a vice president in charge of production for one of the biggest mortgage firms in Texas. But "negotiating" her way into that position was anything but easy.

Fran joined the company as an executive assistant shortly after graduating from a two-year business college. She performed well and was soon promoted to loan processor, a position she held for about 10 years.

Though pay raises came regularly, Fran became concerned about her progress. She was an intelligent, dedicated and ambitious employee, but she began to feel her career had reached a dead end. After all, there were *no* female employees in the company's executive hierarchy, and that would be her next move up the management ladder.

Her Frustration Grows

Fran discussed her problem with the company president several times. But each time, her attempt to negotiate a loftier position ended in frustration. "You're doing a great job where you are," the president said. "Besides, our management people need to know a lot about how we deal with investors." Fran felt a bit like the college graduate who, upon applying for a job, was told, "We want a young college graduate with ten years' experience."

Because of this dilemma. Fran began to find her negotiations with the president increasingly frustrating. Her "underdog" role in these negotiations became more and more pronounced, since she was negotiating from a position of increasing weakness.

It was at this low point in her career that Fran clearly saw the path she would have to take if she were to gain any semblance of parity in future discussions with the president; she would have to find out a great deal more about how her company related with its many investors across the country.

Gaining Expertise in a Hurry

This she began to do systematically. For nearly a year, Fran did her homework thoroughly. She helped entertain—

and picked the brains of—investors when they would visit the home office to inspect local properties; attended finance seminars; took a college course in finance; and all the while, found out all she could about investor relations from within the company.

Fran then prepared a plan that would not only give better service to existing investors, but probably add investors to the company's portfolio.

When the conversation got around to promotion at her next performance review, Fran was loaded for bear. When the talk got down to investor relations, Fran played her trump card. She acted and talked like an expert on investors, and apparently convinced the president she *was* one. Within 30 days, she was promoted to vice president. That's how one underdog came out ahead by becoming supercompetent in her field.

HOW DICK WATSON GAINED LEVERAGE

Dick Watson, now an executive with a major aerospace firm, is another person who liberated himself from a perennial underdog role by become a self-styled expert.

Watson graduated from a technical school. When he joined his company he was assigned to the engineering department, and this is where his negotiating problems began. Watson found it difficult to negotiate a raise, much less a promotion. He frequently had trouble getting his points across to his peers. Watson's main problem was that he was generally thought of as a "technician" and not a fully accredited professional engineer.

Snobbism Is Widespread

This kind of professional snobbism is widespread in business and industry. Nonlawyers, for example, usually find it hard to get recognized in a legal environment. Nonaccountants are rarely held in high esteem in work environments where certified public accountants (CPAs) reign supreme. Anyone with less than a PhD usually finds himself fighting an uphill battle for recognition in the world of academe. All become proverbial underdogs in their negotiations.

And so it was with Watson. He became stereotyped as a technical person rather than an engineer. And despite the fact that he was knowledgeable and talented, he found himself on the short end of most of his negotiations.

"Game Plan" Revealed

So how did Watson break the profession's "snob barrier" and gain a high degree of parity in negotiation? Like Fran Hudson, he developed an effective "game plan" and worked extra hard to execute it.

Watson made his bid at a time when the United States was debating whether to build a commercial supersonic transport. Britain and France were getting ready to launch the Concorde, which would whisk passengers across the Atlantic twice as fast as America's subsonic airliners. Potentially at stake was the country's supremacy in commercial aviation.

Fortunately for Watson, his company was then making the first operational twice-the-speed-of-sound bomber, the B-58 Hustler. And since commercial aircraft are usually developed from experience gained by the military, Watson reasoned, why not use the B-58 experience as a basis for his company's building a commercial transport with similar capability?

The idea was solid, and it caused Watson to launch into a thorough investigation of the possibility of building the nation's first Supersonic Transport (SST).

Research Is Thorough

Watson started in-depth research of every facet of the complex program. He quickly discovered that developing an SST would require a quantum jump in the state of the art.

Would the plane be built of steel or titanium? How fast—Mach 2 or Mach 3? Technology would dictate the speed to an extent. But there was also the matter of how fast the flying public wanted to go. Experts disagreed on virtually every major issue.

After months of such research, Watson put the major issues into focus in an article which was published in a prestigious national trade magazine.

His conclusion: Since the B-58 had gained virtually all the Mach 2 experience gained to date by a large military plane, why not convert a B-58 into an SST prototype and fly it into foreign airports to show America's interest in developing such an aircraft?

Article Attracts Attention

The article created some ripples in aviation, civilian and military circles, but more important, it caused some excitement in Watson's own company. For example, Watson was invited to dine in the company's executive dining room to discuss the article with the management team.

Nothing really ever came of the article. Watson's company never built an SST. But no matter. Through the article, Watson had gained a *reputation* in his own bailiwick for being an astute *professional*. If top brass felt this way, how could Watson's peers feel differently?

The bottom line of all this is that practically over night, Watson became a true power negotiator. He negotiated a promotion and was regarded plantwide as a peer, not an underdog.

Planning Imperative

Becoming totally versed in the subject at hand is vital to a negotiator's success. But it is equally important to develop a workable "game plan" for any given negotiation. You need to plan *what* you're going to say, and precisely *how* you're going to say it.

This would be true, for example, if as head of a citizen's group, you plan to present a park-improvement program to the city council; or, as an executive, you try to sell a new proposal to your board of directors. It would be equally true if you were trying to sell a pension plan to a corporation, or if you as an individual with limited collateral were trying to borrow a sizable sum of money from a bank.

JOHN REEVES BORROWS TO BUILD

John Reeves, a Texas developer, is a case in point. Reeves thinks big and builds big. As a result, he's constantly having to borrow large sums from banks. Acutely aware of his underdog role with bankers, John offsets this disadvantage by preparing his interview to the tiniest detail.

"You have to realize that the banker has every advantage," Reeves says. "He has the money and thus the power to turn you down, somewhat arbitrarily if he so chooses.

"Experience has taught me that a banker invariably wants to know the answer to several basic questions, such as: How much money do I want? For how long? How do I plan to use the money? Specifically, how am I going to pay it back? What happens if my plan goes wrong?"

Questions Carefully Conceived

"Realizing this, I try to answer these questions in my opening pitch. This way, I'm pretty much in control and in many ways dictate the thrust and direction of the interview.

"So after exchanging amenities, I say something like, 'Mr. Banker, my organization would like to buy a new service franchise which is moving into the area. As shown in our audited report, the system has done well on the West Coast and in the Midwest.

" 'We'd like to get a 25-year loan. We plan to pay it back from earnings we get from the franchise. Our business volume is projected on what similar operations have done during their first five years in business. Here's our written projection on this program, which as you can see, has been audited by our accounting firm.' "

Reeves Keeps Control

What has Reeves done thus far in the interview? Two things, at least. First, he's shown that he has really done his home work—the hallmark of a real pro. Second, he has directed the interview the way *he* wants it to go.

Why is preparation so all-important? "The pride you have in your work is reflected in the amount of homework you've done," Reeves continued. "It relates directly to *character*, and with most bankers, this is probably the biggest single asset you have going for you. I'd say it counts as much as 50 percent. Sure, they're interested in cash flow, market conditions and all that. But primarily, they want to know if you're a solid citizen."

Bankers Like Attention

Where does this negotiation take place? Frequently in the bank. But not if Reeves has his way. "Like most other business people, bankers are human," he points out. "They like to be called by their first names and remembered on their birthdays and anniversaries. They're not averse to being wined and dined, providing it's done above board and in good taste." As a result, Reeves usually arranges a luncheon or dinner meeting with his banker at a conservative but highly fashionable spot.

There's one final step in the preparation. What if the banker turns him down? And sometimes, he does.

Alternate Plan Set

If this happens, Reeves switches to his alternate plan, which includes such questions as: "May I ask, what would you do in my place? Maybe I should go to another bank? Which one? Who should I ask for at this bank? What should I tell him? Is it all right if I tell him there's been a change in policy at your bank? What do you plan to tell him?"

Review this line of questioning and I think you will find the banker's answers will enable Reeves to get the banker to tell him exactly how to solve his problem.

Gets Valuable Information

"You see," Reeves says, "bankers like to help you when they can. They normally don't *like* to turn people down. But if I get the answers to my questions, I then know whom to approach and exactly how to approach them. In addition, I'll know what kind of report my original banker is going to give. Thus I have solid information on which to base my interview with the new banker."

Becoming an "expert" and preparing to the hilt for your negotiation are almost certain to help you chuck the role of underdog. Or, at least minimize it!

ACTING CONFIDENTLY

Power negotiators need plenty of confidence, but how do you sustain a high level of confidence when you're the underdog in a negotiation? Well, you have to work very hard at it.

As mentioned earlier, one's aspiration level (in effect, confidence level) typically goes up and down during almost any negotiation. It tends to go up when things are going well and drop when things go badly.

This will hold true, to a degree, for almost any negotiator. But for the bona fide power negotiator, the fluctuations are less extreme. He or she will tend to sustain at least the appearance of having a high confidence level *a good deal of the time.*

How do you develop a high level of confidence? Here are a few techniques that have worked for individuals who have overcome real or imagined handicaps to become legitimate power negotiators.

Act As If You Couldn't Fail

The philosophy of "as if" poses the question: "How would I act . . . what would I do . . . if I *knew* I could not fail?"

Fantasy you say? Everyone fails at one time or another? True, of course. But push pure logic aside for the moment and wrestle with the question: How *would* you act if you knew you could not fail?

Chances are, you would act in a very confident, authoritative manner. You would, in other words, evince the kind of attitude that would stand you in good stead at any negotiation.

"All right," you say, "but what if I act 'as if' and I lose the negotiation anyway? Doesn't this mean that I'm just fooling myself?" Not necessarily. If you had carried your usual underdog attitude into the negotiation, you would no doubt have lost anyway—and will *continue* to lose most of the time. On the other hand, power negotiators tell me that if you act "as if" often enough and long enough you will eventually gain the kind of sustained confidence a power negotiator needs.

Experiences Should Be Used

The "as if" philosophy will usually work best when your outlook is based on real-life experiences. Visualize in detail precisely how you felt the last time you enjoyed a highly successful negotiation. Recall as vividly as possible the details of how you *looked, felt* and *acted* on that occasion. As well as you can remember, what words did you use? What gestures did you make? What kind of preparation led to your success?

Once you have captured this *feeling*—this frame of mind—you are then in the right mental posture to negotiate "as if" you could not lose.

This doesn't mean, of course, that you will win every negotiation. It does mean that you will be in the right frame of mind to win it. Some contend that this approach simply amounts to psyching yourself up. Perhaps so, but what is wrong with getting yourself in the proper frame of mind for any type of encounter, including a negotiation?

How Joe Saylers Sells

Salespeople, for example, are constantly having to get themselves charged up, since they are almost always underdogs when dealing with clients or prospects.

Joe Saylers, for example, sells mainly to upper-level executives. To "minimize" the executive's power position, Joe visualizes him sitting across the desk dressed only in his underwear! "It's a reminder to me," Joe says, "that he has to put his pants on one leg at a time—just like me."

Now technically this little gimmick doesn't necessarily add to Sayler's negotiating ability. But he claims it does help him develop the proper frame of mind for entering the negotiation.

Act "as if" you can't fail as a power negotiator—and many times you cannot.

Act and Talk Like a Power Negotiator

When you're the underdog in a negotiation, *don't* act or talk like it. That's the advice handed down by top power negotiators.

"It's a law of human nature," one veteran arbitrator said. "Once your opponent finds out what you will submit to, he will act accordingly. If he discovers you've entered the negotiation with hat in hand, he's almost sure to interpret this posture as a sign of weakness and try to drive a very hard bargain. On the other hand, if your actions lead him to *think* you are a power negotiator, your odds of gaining parity in the relationship improve greatly.

The solution then is to act and talk like a power

negotiator; to develop a sort of mental toughness. Being *mentally* tough obviously does not mean being rude or overbearing. It does mean having the poise to hold your own in a negotiation, despite the intimidating tactics of a more powerful opponent.

Dealing with an Abusive Client

For example, the purchasing agent for a nationally known department store in Houston has a reputation for being a rough, tough person to deal with. One of his favorite tactics is to verbally assault salespeople in an effort to get price concessions.

Many salespeople, feeling themselves in an inferior position, *do* become victimized by these tactics. When he curses, they cringe. But not Mel Rosenbloom, a veteran salesman who handles a top line of men's sportswear.

Mel listens patiently to the purchasing agent's expletive-laden tirade, then counters mildly with some rough language of his own. "Look," Mel boasts, "I've got the best damned line of men's sportswear you can find anywhere. You and I both know you'd be missing a sure bet if you didn't carry our line."

Mel Knows His Man

Mel's response might sound a bit impertinent, if not risky, but Mel knows his customer. He realizes that the purchasing agent, like many who find themselves in a superior position, uses rough language to intimidate salespeople and gain the upper hand in the negotiation.

Profanity is just one, but a frequently used, way to show "superiority." The way to counter this tactic and in the same breath show you plan to negotiate on an equal footing, is to counter with your own rough language. Mel did and soon found himself negotiating on "equal" terms.

The purchasing agent's use of profanity to intimidate is not uncommon. In so doing, the agent is saying, "I am more powerful than you in this negotiation, and I can use this type of language because I hold the upper hand."

If the recipient of this verbal abuse tolerates it, he puts himself in a definite underdog negotiating stance. He is tacitly admitting his opponent's superiority.

If, on the other hand, he stands up for his professional rights, he relays the message that he is a negotiator to be contended with. This is precisely what Mel does, and this is one of the reasons he comes out ahead in most of his negotiations.

THIRD PARTY CAN HELP

Still another way to combat your underdog status is to enlist the support of a friendly third party, directly or indirectly.

For example, I have a friend who is an incurable hunting enthusiast. Every year near Christmas, he and a few of his buddies go on a week-long hunting trip to Colorado.

Each year, he has to "negotiate" the trip with his wife, who neither shares his enthusiasm for hunting nor appreciates his week-long absence near Christmas.

But my friend is a shrewd person. Rather than negotiate the trip alone, he holds a dinner party several weeks before the trip, inviting all his hunting buddies and their wives. Collectively, the men negotiate their annual fun and games. Sometimes, there is strength in numbers!

Shirley Parks Uses Alumni

Shirley Parks, who heads the annual sustentation drive for a southern university, often enlists the aid of well-known alumni to aid her cause.

When Shirley solicits a donation from a tough-to-handle corporate person, she'll take along a well-known alumnus—an ex-football star or someone who has made it big in the business world or in the arts—to help her negotiate. The tactic apparently works, for Shirley usually gets more donations than any other worker.

Getting Indirect Support

There is also the indirect support, which is frequently used by salespeople. This support is customarily in the form of letters of testimony from satisfied customers telling what a fine job the salesperson has done for them.

Some contend that such letters are self-serving, overly dramatic and sometimes "rigged." Nonetheless, they remain one of the salesperson's most potent ways of proving his or her point. It would be best to have that satisfied customer on hand. But that's impractical in most cases, so the next best thing is his "testimony."

Negotiating as an underdog is an uphill battle. But the real power negotiator can usually find some way to even the score with his more powerful adversary.

Chapter 12

USING POWER NEGOTIATION TO GET A BETTER JOB

Chances arc, you'll spend about one fourth of your life working. Little wonder, then, that trying to land a job that "fits" your temperament and talents should rank as one of your top-priority negotiations.

Unfortunately, only a comparative handful seem to be able to swing this negotiation successfully. A national survey showed that only four of ten business and professional people are "well adjusted" in their jobs. Most private placement counsellors claim this sort of occupational discontent is much more widespread.

Why the Grass Looks Greener

Why the problem? There are, no doubt, as many reasons as there are disgruntled employees: low pay, bad management, poor location, and a host of real and imagined personal grievances. The list is virtually endless!

Then, too, there is the perennial problem of an employee reaching the "height of a mediocre career." Though almost always uttered in jest, the observation is often true enough. It *is* awfully crowded at the top; and many *are* called and few *are* chosen for the executive suite.

Thus we have the universal dilemma of many top-notch people working in jobs that require only a fraction of their talents. These people are not able to self-actualize—live up to the best within themselves—as famed behavioral psychologist Abraham Maslow put it.

WHICH ROUTE TO TAKE?

So what can *you* do to safeguard against getting bogged down in this morass of professional mediocrity? For starters, you can learn to use power negotiating tactics and techniques to find that right job.

The strategy you'll use will naturally depend on your unique situation. If you want to move up in your own company, your goal is "simple": you mainly need to find ways to gain *greater visibility*.

If you're planning to go to another outfit, it becomes another ball game. You can act on your own behalf, or you can put your fate in the hands of a competent third party. First, let's take a look at how a few power negotiators have succeeded on their own.

Help Solve a Problem

Gaining visibility within your own company means somehow rising above the pack. One of the most effective ways of doing this, according to George E. Watson, director of the Bryant Bureau, an executive placement company in Dallas, is to help your company solve some of its major problems.

Watson recalls one such instance when he was serving as president of one of Anaconda's major divisions. "We were finding it increasingly hard to make timely decisions because of data-transmission problems," he said. "Too much time was lost between the time information arrived at our plant and the time it was passed on to our sales locations in the field."

Salesman Submits Viable Plan

Watson called a meeting of his key executives and their staff support people to seek solutions to the problem. He gave each person at the session "up to 10 minutes" to outline his or her solution. Though many good ideas emerged, one presentation in particular—from a sales representative—was clearly so well conceived and organized that Watson asked the presentor to stay after the regular meeting ended.

"I congratulated him on his *detailed* plan to install a nationwide data-transmission system," Watson recalled. "In our discussion, I discovered that he had been working on the plan for nearly a year, mostly on his own time."

Need a Problem? Look Around!

"I immediately appointed him chairman of a committee to follow through on the plan, being especially careful to compliment this man's supervisor on the wonderful way in which he was 'developing his people.' That employee, incidentally, is on his way to becoming one of the key executives in the company."

How do you spot problems within your company? Just keep your eyes and ears open. Problems abound in most organizations, just waiting for a power negotiator to solve them. And the beauty of it is, the problem need not relate to your immediate area. The salesman who solved Watson's problem was only marginally involved in data-transmission and scheduling.

Writing for Recognition

Writing an article for a leading trade, or even popular, magazine can frequently gain you the desired visibility in your company. In an earlier chapter, we mentioned the "technician" who gained recognition not only from his co-workers, mostly engineers, but from top management as well for his perceptive article on the supersonic transport.

Susan Davenport, a marketing analyst for a business system company, is another case in point. Susan developed a software program which her company was marketing—with only modest success—to the hotel/motel industry. However, the program *had* been sold to a nationally known motel chain, which was using the system with a high degree of success.

Sales Go Up After Publication

Susan researched the hotel's operation thoroughly, then wrote an article showing how her company's system was being used. The article was published—in fact, got cover-page recognition—in a national motel trade magazine. After that, sales increased dramatically.

Management rewarded Susan with a healthy raise, and the following year, a promotion. Perhaps even more important to Susan, she got recognition which she had been unable to gain during five years with the organization.

How do you go about placing an article in a reputable trade publication? Probably the best way is to write the editor directly and ask if he's interested. Most trade publications *welcome* good story ideas about happenings within their industry.

How Randy Davis Gained Visibility

No doubt about it, you can, if you're capable, literally talk your way to success in a negotiation. Randy Davis did.

Randy was a first-line supervisor in the quality control department of a big manufacturing plant which handled mostly defense contracts. When his company launched a value engineering (VE) program aimed at making all manufacturing processes cost effective, Randy volunteered to design and put on the company's in-house seminar.

Davis's initial efforts at teaching were anything but outstanding. He had had limited platform experience, and his material needed beefing up. To help rectify this situation, Davis helped form a Toastmaster's International Club in his company. Within a few months, his speaking ability improved dramatically.

Efforts Are Rewarded

Before long, Davis was in demand not only locally, but nationwide as a speaker on value engineering. He later put on a VE seminar at the University of Wisconsin, where he was given an almost perfect rating by his peers.

Understandably, it was almost impossible for this type of effort to go unrecognized in Davis's own company. And it didn't. Within a year, he was promoted to a newly created spot as director of value engineering, a department which was to carry considerable clout in the company.

Make Sure You're Good

Speaking can be a double-edged sword. A good speech can lead to fame and fortune, but a bad one can be counter-productive. I recall, for example, where a particularly poor presentation got a personnel executive "barred" from future appearances before the board of directors. And shortly after that, the executive was shunted off to a dead-end spot in the corporate structure.

If you decide to go the speaking route, do as Davis did. Prepare thoroughly, and if you find yourself wanting in speaking ability, take steps to correct this problem before you start gaining visibility via the spoken word.

Conventional Methods Work Too

These are some of the more dramatic ways of gaining additional visibility in your organization. You can put in lots of overtime, making sure your boss knows precisely how much time you've logged. Many executives, despite some "technical" shortcomings, manage to gain visibility by showing up at the right time and the right place. Whatever tack you take, be

nice to everybody on the way up; you might meet them on the
way down.

GEORGE WATSON SEES BOTH SIDES

Perhaps a majority of people who are seeking greener
occupational pastures do so outside their present company.
Some pursue this task on their own, but in increasing numbers, job seekers are going through third-party executive-
placement agencies, colloquially called "headhunters."

George Watson, former Anaconda executive who is currently head of the Bryant Bureau in Dallas, feels much of his
success can be attributed to his being able to "work both sides
of the fence."

"The first thing a competent third party has going for
him is objectivity," Watson said. "We are completely *unemo-
tional* about a person's changing jobs. The typical job seeker,
on the other hand, often regards a change—or even a
transfer—as traumatic. This tends to affect his judgment and
sometimes causes him to take untimely or ill-conceived actions
which can seriously impair his negotiating ability."

Salary Offer Stymies Talks

For example, a young engineer who was making $29,000
a year applied for a job that seemed "right down my alley."
The interview went well and concluded with the applicant
asking the interviewer what the job would pay.

"It pays $30,000 to start," the interviewer said, "and
there's a real chance to advance rapidly if you can produce."
"Sorry," the engineer replied. "I couldn't change for less than
$33,000."

At this point, for practical purposes, the negotiation
came to an end, mainly because of the last-and-final-offer
stance of the interviewer and the attendant emotional reaction of the young engineer.

By quoting a *firm* $30,000 figure, the interviewer in effect "locked in" the company's position. If he had yielded to the applicant's demand for $33,000, he would have admitted that he was lying, or at the least, playing games. Further, he probably would have held a grudge which might have affected the applicant's position later on.

Nor would the applicant likely have been *totally* satisfied with $33,000. "If they offered me $33,000," he would have thought, "why not $35,000, or even more?" Quite often in such cases, the applicant leaves thinking he's left something on the table—that he could have gotten more.

Third Party Success Likely

Could the negotiation have been successfully concluded by a competent third party? Chances are, it could. And therein lies the strength of an objective third party. He or she can perform roughly the same function as a mediator in resolving a touchy management-labor union squabble.

It is this ability to thoroughly understand both parties and both sides of the issues that often enables a qualified placement counsellor to settle the negotiation amicably—and profitably—for both parties. Equally important, he or she can negotiate so that all parties emerge with their self-esteem intact. And remember, everybody needs to get *something* from a negotiation.

Getting a 50 Percent Raise

There is still another very practical reason for selecting a competent third party to help you land a top job. The third party can, if circumstances are right, get you a bigger raise in pay than you could have gotten for yourself.

"Normally," Watson said, "you can expect to get a raise of from 10 to 15 percent when you change jobs. Anything above this is the exception. However, I've been able to get a few of my clients as much as a 50 percent pay hike. This has been mostly in cases where the employee has been habitually underpaid and where he or she happens to be underutilized.

Unfortunately, both conditions exist to some degree today in business and industry."

Such a situation existed with a client whom we'll call Brenda. Brenda had served for a number of years with a management consultant firm in the Southwest. She was attracted to Watson's firm by a "consulting job" which paid "up to $35,000."

Brenda Holds Out for More

After a series of interviews, Watson concluded that Brenda should be one of the five finalists for the job; in fact, she was *his* odds-on favorite for the assignment. Brenda boasted top professional and academic credentials and had a fine "track record" in her field.

But one major problem cropped up. Brenda, who was making $24,000, insisted on a starting salary of $30,000. This salary, she figured, certainly was commensurate with others in the field. However, the district manager of the firm's Dallas office would go only as high as $27,000, arguing logically that this would represent a "more than decent raise for her."

Watson Approaches Corporate Boss

Watson explained to the Dallas district manager that Brenda was being underpaid by her present employer and that she would not consider anything under $30,000. But the Dallas manager stood firm in his position. The matter would have ended there had Watson not pursued the issue further.

He called the firm's president, a personal friend, in his client's New York City headquarters and explained the situation. "This lady is the best qualified applicant I have," he said, "and she's perfectly justified in holding out for $30,000. In reality, she's worth more than that. You're going to lose a top prospect if your Dallas manager sticks to that $27,000 figure."

"I understand," the president said. "Just let me handle it." He did, and the Dallas manager hired the lady at $30,000.

Why a Third Party Works

It is doubtful if Brenda could have landed this job on her own—at least at her price. But an effective third party like Watson can serve as a catalyst and make things happen for several reasons.

First, he is a highly skilled interviewer, capable of "sizing up" an applicant objectively and comparing him or her with others in the field.

Second, Watson knows the wage and organizational structure of the industries in which he specializes. In this case, for example, he knew that Brenda's counterparts in the Omaha and Atlanta branch offices made considerably higher salaries. And the New York representative made even more. Such knowledge enables him to negotiate from strength.

Third, he was able to use his personal contacts within the industry (all good headhunters have them). In Watson's case, it was the corporate president in New York, who was instrumental in getting Brenda hired.

And there is still another reason, only marginally applicable in this case, why it can be wise to enlist the aid of a third party. It is an unwritten law in management circles that top executives don't look for jobs; jobs look for them. "Theoretically," Watson said, "top executives benefit most from third parties, since this puts them in the position of 'surveying the field' or 'considering offers' rather than job hunting."

Biggest Increases Come in Selling

The most dramatic salary increases usually come in the selling and marketing areas, which often have overrides and incentive plans that make the higher salaries possible.

Watson's value to an applicant in such situations is in being familiar with the company and knowing what others are making in that company. "For example," Watson said, "I had an applicant who hadn't made over $30,000 in his life in selling. I sent him to an oil supply company that offered him a base salary of $18,000, plus commissions and overrides.

"He didn't want to accept, which meant that I had another selling job on my hands," Watson said. "Sizing up this man's track record in selling and knowing what others had made with this same company, I assured him he would be making $40,000 within two years. I was wrong! He made $60,000 his *first* year with the company."

How a Professor Got a Big Raise

What are the biggest problems most job seekers have? "Many overestimate their own worth," Watson said. "On the other hand, quite a few applicants are incapable of recognizing a *real* opportunity when they see one. This is especially true when it comes to starting salaries.

"For example," Watson continued, "I recently represented a college professor who had just completed 11 years of teaching at the University of Mississippi. He had his doctorate degree and was making about $26,000 a year. Now that's not a bad salary for a college professor with his experience, but this fellow felt he should be making as much as his classmates who had gone into industry—about $40,000 to $50,000. Naturally, he was disappointed when a major chemical company offered him a starting salary of $28,000.

Makes Move into Management

"He was on the verge of declining the offer when I finally convinced him he ought to accept the offer for a couple of reasons. First, he would have to make the transition from college to industry *somewhere*. And second, this was a logical place to make it—with a blue-chip company that was willing to pay for top performance."

Fortunately, things *did* work out. Within two years, he had bridged the gap between college and industry, and he was on the verge of moving into middle management. His salary goals were then clearly in sight.

How to Negotiate Your Salary

Negotiating salary can be ticklish, even for the pros. Many job seekers shoot too high and talk themselves out of what might have been a great opportunity. Perhaps even more aim too low and soon find themselves disenchanted in a job where they are underpaid and underutilized.

How should an applicant respond if the interviewer asks, "What kind of salary are you looking for?" "I tell my clients that this is really too personal an issue to negotiate," Watson said. "It's an impossible question and I recommend that my people respond with a question of their own, such as, 'Mr. Employer, I'm sure you have a value on the job. Do you mind my asking what that salary range might be?' "

"Almost every job in every company has a definite economic value," Watson said. "The company cannot normally go above this range for fear of ruining the salary structure of jobs above that range. If they go too low, they end up with a dissatisfied employee. So my advice is to use one of the salesperson's favorite tactics for controlling an interview: answer a question with a question. You have little to lose and possibly much to gain by doing so."

RÉSUMÉ GETS FOOT IN DOOR

Whether you seek a better opportunity on your own or use a competent third party, you'll need a professionally written résumé to help you get your foot in the door.

"Many highly qualified applicants for a job—sometimes the *best* qualified—never get to the interview stage because of a poorly written résumé," Watson said. "For this reason, we insist that each of our clients follow a specific format that is tried and proven."

This format calls for a résumé that is comprehensive, yet concise—never over one or two pages in length.

Most companies are interested in *who* you are and *what* you've done. Obviously these factors must be emphasized, but succinctly!

Speak to Company's Interests

What the company is even more interested in is what you can do for them. So tell them, and back it up with examples, such as: "Organized, trained and developed a ten-man sales force that had an annual production of $750,000," or "Managed a training department that developed and presented management and sales seminars nationwide under an $875,000 budget."

"Don't be modest," Watson said. "Your résumé should be an unabashed attempt to 'sell' yourself. If it tiptoes, if it's nervously modest, if it hedges, if it whispers timidly—it will fail. It may fail in any event, but at least it won't fail for want of trying. Make them an offer they can't refuse!"

Seven Steps to Follow

Here, in Watson's opinion, are the seven most common mistakes made in résumés:

1. *They're too wordy.* Read over your résumé and eliminate every word that doesn't carry its weight. Then give it the "bore test." Read it to a friend and if he's not interested, find out why. Then *rewrite* it.

2. *They list salary requirements.* Why do most big corporations fail to list salaries when they run an ad for a job opening? Because they've learned that for most offers, the salary will appear low in relation to the job or to a competitive offer. You run the same risk in listing a salary. Remember, the résumé's job is to get you an interview, not a salary!

3. *They're 'me-oriented'.* Avoid phrases such as, "My objective is . . ." Again, the company is more interested in what you can do for them. And be specific: make them more

money, increase efficiency, gain a greater share of the market, avoid labor problems, and so forth.

4. *They assume too much reader comprehension.* No reflection on the reader's intelligence quotient. It simply means that he usually has neither the time nor the inclination to piece all the unrelated facts together. If, for example, you're basically an accountant but can run a division, or a chemist who can do marketing, say so.

5. *They're confusing and contain too much information.* If you're at once a doctor, lawyer, engineer and sales executive, believe it or not you have a problem. The *reader* will be confused by all your talents. The idea is to zero in on one or two of your main talents and sell these.

6. *They use stiff, formal language.* Don't be flip, of course, but make it highly *readable.* Use short words, short sentences and short paragraphs. Sprinkle your résumé with personal pronouns. Use mainly the active rather than the passive voice ("I believe" rather than "It is believed"). And by all means delete unnecessary words. Use white space generously.

7. *They include too much personal information.* Married? Divorced? Active in your church? No church affiliation at all? The point is, who cares? At least at this point in time. Stating personal information more often than not knocks you out of an interview. If the employee is interested, he'll ask these questions in the interview, but government regulations limit him to the number of questions he can ask.

Negotiating a job is too serious to handle in an off-hand manner. Either develop an expertise of your own or call on a competent third party to do the job for you.

Chapter 13

USING POWER NEGOTIATION IN SELLING

The stereotype of a traveling salesman—Willy Loman making the circuit on a smile and a shoeshine—has changed dramatically during the past generation.

To be sure, the smile and shoeshine are still there. But today's professional salesperson operates in a more sophisticated work environment. He or she needs to be better informed and better trained; in fact, needs to possess all the traits and skills of a successful power negotiator, including:

- A positive attitude and attendant high aspiration level, which is especially crucial to the salesperson.

- Highly developed communication skills—the ability to talk, listen and question *expertly*.

- An understanding of *power*; how to use it, and how to cope with it when in an underdog role, which is a typical role for salespeople.

- A working knowledge of negotiating power tactics and techniques, such as *patience, limited authority, dead-*

line, take-it-or-leave-it, lowballing, highballing, withdrawal, and others.

CLOSING IS BOTTOM LINE

We've discussed all these points as they relate to negotiating in general. In this chapter, you'll want to bring them to bear on the salesperson's ultimate success in negotiation—making the sale.

Making that sale usually depends on the salesperson's being able to successfully complete three steps:

- Discovering the prospect's basic buying motive, or need.

- Overcoming objections.

- Closing the transaction.

Using all the negotiating skills and tactics we've discussed, let's take a look at how top salespeople get the business.

FINDING THE PROSPECT'S PROBLEM

Step 1—Discovering the prospect's basic buying motive, or need, or, to put it another way, pinpointing his problem.

Make no mistake, the prospect is interested in *his* problem. So much so, in fact, that he has very likely built up what some salespeople call a "preoccupation barrier," an obstacle which you must normally penetrate before you can gain his undivided attention.

Often, there is another obstacle to overcome: the "trust barrier." The prospect—like you—has been conditioned from youth to be wary of salespeople. In Economics 101 you were made aware of *caveat emptor:* let the buyer beware.

And beyond these two barriers is the problem of adjusting your personality to the client's.

At a minimum, these are all problems, or barriers, you'll have to contend with before you can start to negotiate successfully with a prospect. It takes skill, knowledge (and sometimes luck) to overcome these barriers. But overcome them you must if you're to emerge as a salesperson with strong power negotiation skills.

So what's the answer? How do you break down these barriers? Specifically, how do you deal with the preoccupation problem? The answer is deceptively simple: you address yourself to the prospect's problem; you talk to *his* interests right away.

How Joe Petrovich Does It

Joe Petrovich, a top small-business-computer salesman, is a past master at establishing this kind of rapport with prospects. Before meeting with the decision maker, Joe finds out everything he can about the business: number of employees, sales volume, growth plans—anything that might give Joe ammunition for his sales interview. He is especially on the lookout for any problems the business might have at the moment.

Where does he get this kind of information? Anywhere he can—from Dun and Bradstreet, trade associations, Chambers of Commerce, business associations, and even employees themselves if he can find a way to do so. And what does he do with this information? When possible, he uses it to help him break the prospect's preoccupation barrier.

For example, Joe was able to get considerable information, including financial data, from the controller of a small wholesale distributor he was about to call on. The owner of the distributorship was Sid Levine, who had a reputation for being rough on salespeople.

Dealing with Sid Levine

Because of Sid's reputation, Joe planned his interview even more carefully than usual, even down to exchanging pleasantries. He would mention the Dallas Cowboys, a football team Sid had followed from its entry into professional football.

Joe did manage to use this icebreaker successfully in the interview, then came right to the point: "Mr. Levine, you've got a very profitable organization. But I know how you can make it even more profitable."

"Oh?"

"Right now, you're losing at least $10,000 a year—and that's a conservative estimate—by not taking advantage of the two percent discount for early payment of most of your bills. In addition, you're losing money on your accounts receivable by not getting rid of bad debts in time. Let's say about $5,000 here. But your biggest loss is in your inventory: Lost sales by not having high-priority items on board and in using costly storage space for slow-moving items. Perhaps you're losing as much as $5,000 more a year here. Using our System 20/50, Mr. Levine, you can save about $25,000 the first year—*even after paying for the system!*"

Getting a Commitment

"Where did you get all those figures?"

"You were kind enough to let me talk with your controller. Remember?"

"Yeah."

"Mr. Levine, if I can prove to your satisfaction that I *can* save you this $25,000 the first year, and at the same time make your operation more efficient and profitable, will you let me install the system today?"

"Well, maybe. Let me see what you've got."

Has Joe broken through Sol Levine's preoccupation barrier? Indeed he has. He has grabbed the prospect's attention, and he can be reasonably certain that his presentation will be heard. If he can prove his point, he's probably got himself a sale, due at least in part to his being able to zero in on his prospect's problem early in the interview.

Questioning Is the Key

Joe obviously isn't always able to get this much information beforehand. Most of his interviews are more "impromptu"; he gains the information he needs through effective interviewing techniques. And most successful interviews, you'll recall, are based on being able to ask the "right" questions. Quite often, many key questions can be planned beforehand.

Since the key to this negotiation is in being able to find and solve the prospect's problem, Joe tries to get the prospect to talk as soon—and as much—as he can. He usually sets the pace for the negotiation with this question: "Mr. Prospect, do you mind if I ask you a few questions about your business at the outset? It'll help me determine if my company's program can fit your needs."

Joe feels this line of questioning accomplishes two things. It asks "permission" to ask questions about the prospect's business, thus minimizing the chances that the prospect will feel his privacy is being invaded. Further, it usually gives the prospect the feeling that the interview is being tailored to *his* specific needs. In other words, he's going to get a "tailored" rather than a "canned" sales presentation.

Getting Prospects to Talk

Having established a good working relationship, Joe zeros in as quickly as possible on the prospect's problem. Realizing that he will be unable to find the prospect's problem so long as *he* is talking, Joe gets the prospect to talking as soon as possible through well-planned indirect, or open-end questions.

Direct questions, you'll recall, usually elicit a "Yes" or "No" answer, which puts the ball back in the salesperson's court. Indirect questions, on the other hand, usually prompt the prospect to open up and, in the process, reveal his business problems.

For example, a direct question might be, "Mr. Prospect, are you having any problems with your accounting system?" The prospect *could* give you a rundown on his problems. However, the question is more likely to draw a "No" for a couple of reasons. The prospect might not be able to articulate his problems, or, as sometimes happens, he might become intimidated by your *presuming* that he does have problems and lapse into a noncommunicative posture.

Indirect Query Triggers Conversation

Let's try another approach, this time with an indirect question: "Mr. Prospect, how are you handling your accounts payable?"

"Well," he is likely to reply, "Sally, our bookkeeper, gathers all the bills as they come in and puts them in our accounts payable voucher. Then as soon after the first of the month as possible, she gets them all together and pays the bills. Sometimes it's a little after the first before she can get around to it because she's busy and has some other things to do . . ." And on the prospect goes.

Mission Accomplished

Now Joe can clearly see the problem. Levine is missing out on a high percentage of discounts because his bookkeeper has no way of determining when the bills must be paid to get the discount.

Thence to a more direct question: "Mr. Levine, thank you very much for this valuable information. If I could show you a way to pay at least 50 to 60 percent of these bills on time and save the discount—maybe as much as $5,000 a year— would you be interested in installing our system today?"

Like most prospects under similar circumstances, Levine is likely to answer with a qualified "Yes." "I might be," he says, "if you can prove it."

OVERCOMING OBJECTIONS WITHOUT ARGUING

Step 2—Overcoming Objections. Power negotiators usually' succeed to the extent they can impose their views on others, while defending their own position against their opponents' protestations. These protests, or *objections* as they are called in selling, must normally be overcome before a salesperson can successfully complete the negotiation.

This is so mainly because objections tend to be argumentative in nature, and as every professional salesperson soon learns, it's usually "fatal" to argue with a customer.

"There are essentially two ways to keep arguments to a minimum when answering objections," said Ray Waddington, manager of a Dallas-based sales force. "One is to soften the objection with a buffer statement; the other is to convert the objection into a question.

How a Buffer Can Help

"For example, assume that a prospect says, 'Thanks for an interesting presentation, but I think I'm going to have to pass. Your system is just more than I can afford.'

"Let's assume further that the salesperson responds with 'I disagree, Mr. Prospect; I've proven to you that you desperately need my system, and your financial report shows you definitely *can* afford it.'"

Though accurate, the salesperson's response undoubtedly irritates the prospect. It is very likely to lead to a yes-you-can, no-you-can't argument, which the salesperson is almost certain to lose.

However, note how it sounds when the salesperson responds to the same objection with a buffer statement: "Mr. Prospect, I understand exactly how you feel, and you *do* have a legitimate point. However, let me point out . . ." And so forth.

Agreeing with the Prospect

What effect did the buffer have? It softened the response. It told the prospect, "I understand exactly how you feel, and I can appreciate your concern."

Some experts contend that such a statement hurts the salesperson's cause because it reinforces a negative statement—the objection. However, I feel these critics miss the point. The salesperson is not necessarily agreeing with the prospect's objection; he is simply agreeing with the prospect's *right* to raise it. The buffer simply lays the groundwork for a plausible response, in which the salesperson will attempt to offset the objection by stressing the *benefits* his system offers.

Nor does a buffer statement have to be elaborate. A simple "I understand," often reflects appropriate empathy and appreciably softens the response.

Clarifying with a Question

The second point is to clarify the objection and at the same time rephrase it in the form of a question.

Clarification is important. It lets you know whether you and the prospect are seeing eye to eye on the issues.

Frequently, objections turn out to be mere put-offs. Thus a clarifying question can help you judge whether an objection is valid.

The idea of putting the objection in question form is also psychologically sound. By definition, *overcoming* an objection carries with it the idea of "proving" the prospect is wrong. But answering a prospect's question connotes something entirely different. It puts you in the position of simply *responding* to a legitimate query. Answering a question, in other words, is less likely to lead to an argument than *overcoming* an objection.

Getting the Real Objection

For example, a home owner says to a Realtor, "I'll probably list with you eventually. However, I'm going to hold off for awhile, what with the market being down and selling costs being so high right now."

The objection is rather vague. But see what happens when the salesman clarifies the issue, then puts the objection in *question* form.

"I understand, Mr. Prospect. You feel that because of the high prevailing discount points, you won't be able to net what you want out of your property. Is that correct?"

"Well, yes, I suppose so," the owner responds. "After I pay those darned points on top of the commission and all, there just won't be that much left for me."

What has the salesperson done? He has clarified the question and zeroed in on the real objection: The seller doesn't want to pay discount points. In addition, he has turned the objection into a question, which he will at .npt to "answer."

Closing on a Question

A logical extension of this scenario would be for the salesperson to use still another question to get the seller's commitment. For example: "Mr. Prospect, if I could show you where you could still net a handsome profit from your home despite having to pay discount points, would you be willing to go ahead and list it now?"

"Perhaps," the owner says, "but I'm not sure I know exactly what you mean."

"Let me work out some closing costs for you and show you exactly what you will get if you go FHA, VA and Conventional. Then you can make up your mind. All right?"

"Well, I suppose so. When can you show me those figures?"

"Right now."

FEAR MAKES CLOSING DIFFICULT

Step 3—Closing the Transaction. Probably the most critical step in any negotiation is the close, in which the prospect either accepts or rejects your product or proposition.

Closing is generally considered to be the most difficult step in the sales cycle. Why? I think the clear consensus is: Salespeople fear rejection. In many cases, they have not learned to distinguish between *failing* and *failure*, which is roughly the difference between *fact* and *opinion*.

For example, a salesperson says, "I had a horrible year; I'm a failure." *That* is opinion, based on one year's experience. The *fact* is, he did have a bad year and he did fail during that period. But he becomes a failure only if he has a long succession of failings, and *only if he fails to try again*.

To Close Is to Risk Failing

Many feel the first step in becoming a successful closer in any negotiation is to realize that you *risk failing* (but *not* failure) every time you try to close a sale.

After developing the proper mental attitude about closing, the next step is to develop a repertoire of closing tactics and techniques. You'll want to develop several techniques for a couple of reasons. First, all techniques won't work on all prospects. Second, some of the tactics won't match your personality.

Keeping this in mind, let's take a look at some closing techniques which have worked well for top salespeople.

HIGH ASPIRATION LEVEL NEEDED

Assumptive technique. Simply *assume* that the client is going to buy your product or idea. This technique should be relatively easy to master for the salesperson who has a high aspiration level, which, you'll recall, is characteristic of a successful power negotiator.

The assumptive technique combines a positive state of mind with a questioning technique called the choice-between-two-positives.

For example, a salesman reflects a positive state of mind when he uses the phrase, "*when* you buy" rather than "*if* you buy." He becomes even more positive when he asks, "May I set

up an appointment for 6 p.m., or would a little later—say 8
o'clock—be more convenient?" or, "Would you prefer the
blue or the maroon model?" or, "Would you prefer to use our
convenient lease plan or buy the system under our cash plan?"

Using a Choice-Between-Two-Positives

This is the choice-between-two-positives questioning tactic in action. It works quite well in getting a positive response
from a prospect because of a fundamental law of human
nature. Most people are reluctant to make big decisions, and
many even shy away from making smaller ones. The "little
question" makes it much easier for the party to say "Yes."

For example, if you give a person a choice between something and nothing ("Do you wish to make the purchase or
not?"), he will tend to take nothing.

You make it infinitely easier for him if you give him a
choice between something and something ("Blue or gold?
Tuesday or Wednesday? One or two?"). In a surprising
number of cases, he will take *one* of the two positives.

Another reason the system works is because of what I call
the "law of suggestibility." Next time you're having lunch with
a group, observe how difficult it is for most of the people in
the group to make up their minds. And when they do finally
make a decision, see if they don't order what someone else in
the group "suggests."

HOME BUYER CHANGES PLANS

Future-Event Technique. A newly married couple had
planned to buy a home about a year hence, after they had had
time to consolidate their finances. Meanwhile, they decided
to "shop around" to see what was available in the housing
market.

In shopping, however, they came across one home that
both immediately "fell in love with." They vacillated on
whether to buy, but logic finally prevailed and they decided to
stick to their original plan and wait a year.

Realizing the couple wanted the home badly, the real estate saleslady tried to close with the future-event tactic. Armed with interesting statistics, she called on the couple the next day. "I know how much you like that home," she said, "so I just thought I'd pass on some news that I'm sure you'll be interested in."

Price Increase Promised

"We've just gotten next year's price schedule, and as you can see, this home is going to cost $5,000 more effective January 1. What's more, we have it on good word from the mortgage people that interest rates are almost certain to increase—at least by one percent and maybe even more.

"My point is, you folks could *save* a flat $5,000 if you were to buy that home today. And the amount you would save in paying the lower interest rate would add appreciably to the amount you'd pay over the life of the loan. I'd say several thousand dollars on a 30-year loan. Why don't you come on over and take one more look and let's see what we can work out?"

The couple did look again, and this time they made a down payment on the home. What changed their mind? Probably the *threat of losing* $5,000 outright, and perhaps thousands more in interest payments.

Indeed, the threat of losing something is a strong inducement to buy and serves as foundation for an effective technique for closing a negotiation.

USING REFERRALS TO ADVANTAGE

Referral technique. I recently called on three companies to give me a bid on ridding my home of termites.

There wasn't a great deal of difference in their presentations. All had slick sales pitches, backed up by handsome brochures. Each offered roughly the same warranty, and each agreed to handle the work expeditiously.

Further, there wasn't a great deal of difference in the

price they quoted. I *did* select the low bidder, but not solely for that reason. The main reason was that the company I chose offered me something the other two didn't. He gave me the names—and telephone numbers—of at least a half dozen "satisfied customers" he had serviced in my immediate neighborhood during the past year.

I called one of the referrals, a casual acquaintance who lived down the street, and got a highly favorable report on the company's work. Then and there, I decided to go with this company.

Testimonial Letters Effective

There is nothing better than word-of-mouth advertising, and this is precisely why the referral technique works so well. A good word from someone whom you trust is at least as good as a slick television or newspaper ad—and usually, much better.

One variation of the referral closing technique is the letter of testimony mentioned in an earlier chapter. These are letters from satisfied clients who appreciated your service. Even though the prospect might not "buy" your letter completely, there's a good chance the letter will produce a positive influence—consciously or subconsciously. The latter is important, since psychologists maintain a good many decisions to buy are made subliminally.

Still, perhaps the most effective referral technique is that used by the termite company representative. Give your prospects the names of satisfied customers with whom you think they can relate, and you just might be on the road to closing that transaction.

USING PHYSICAL ACTION

Action technique. This technique combines an assumptive attitude with physical action. It is a technique that Jerry Singer, a business forms salesman, uses with signal success.

One of Jerry's favorite approaches is to guide the interview to a point where delivery date becomes a key issue. Whereupon, he will say, "Mr. Prospect, because of our heavy backlog, we can't normally promise delivery in that short a time. However, I just *might* be able to work you in ahead of another project I'm aware of which doesn't have too high a priority. Let me borrow your phone for just a minute, and I'll find out if I can make the arrangement."

How Insurance Agent Uses the Technique

If the prospect does *not* stop Jerry from completing the call, Jerry figures—quite logically—that he can go ahead and write up the order. That's the key to this technique: Start a physical action of some sort, and if the prospect doesn't stop you, you can *assume* you've got the business.

Many top insurance salespeople use this technique with varying degrees of success. They will ask questions throughout the interview, mostly about family and financial matters. As the prospect answers, the agent jots down answers on a sheet of paper that *appears* to be a questionnaire. Actually, it's the contract, and when the agent finishes the interview, he merely hands the contract over to the prospect and asks him to "authorize the agreement."

The insurance agent has an advantage in using this technique over most other salespeople in that he requires a certain amount of detailed information before he can properly assess the prospect's "insurance needs." Most other salespeople have to use the technique more boldly.

Phrasing a Closing Question

Where such information is not required, the salesperson simply "starts writing" when he is ready to close the negotiation. He does so by asking such questions as, "What is your middle initial?" or, "Do you spell out your middle name or just use the initial?" Again, if the prospect does not stop the salesperson from writing, he can assume the deal has been successfully closed.

This is one of the more aggressive means of capping a

negotiation and must be used at the right *time*, and with the right person, to be effective. Executed prematurely or on a prospect who is already paranoid about being "high-pressured," the technique can backfire.

SEEKING SOMETHING FOR NOTHING

Inducement technique. Contests in which the public stands to win anything from a pot holder to a three-week vacation in Europe have become highly popular in this country. So have "free" weekends to country resorts, and even foreign countries.

Why are such promotional campaigns often successful? Because there lingers in the public's collective breast a strong desire to get *something for nothing*.

For example, I know a builder who constructed homes on four vacant lots near a major high school on a main thoroughfare. The lots had remained vacant for several years because they obviously were the least desirable in the area. Still, my friend built the homes and priced them competitively with comparable homes in a more desirable location not too far away. Despite these disadvantages, the builder sold all four homes within 90 days—an excellent record for this type home.

How Builder Uses the Technique

Later, I discovered how he did it. When prospects showed genuine interest, but balked because of the price or the location, the builder made them an offer they couldn't turn down. "Look," he said, "you like the home and I don't blame you for being concerned about not wanting to go through planting a new yard again. But I'll tell you what I'll do. If you sign a contract today, I'll plant your front yard and back yard solid in St. Augustine grass, and spot-plant the side. In addition, I'll throw in a couple of 10-foot trees. What do you say?"

Four prospects said yes. Why? Mainly, I think, because

they genuinely felt they were getting something for nothing—a *free* yard. Perhaps they were. But my guess is that the
builder had the cost of the yard factored into the total cost of
the homes.

Because people do like bargains, the inducement
technique is quite often an effective closer.

Master these three steps of effective sales negotiation—
discovering the prospect's needs, overcoming his objections,
and closing the transactions—and you'll be on your way to
being able to use power negotiation in selling.

Chapter **14**

USING
POWER NEGOTIATION
AS A BUYER

Purchasing a car represents the height of frustration for many buyers. Prices seem to vary—sometimes markedly—from dealer to dealer. There appears to be no *fixed* price allowed for your trade-ins. Comparing one model with another usually leads to an apples-and-oranges comparison. And to top things off, you are likely to be subjected to low-balling tactics; dealers quote you a low price to get you hooked, then raise the ante once you're ready to buy.

All of this puts the buyer, at least in this instance, in an extremely poor negotiating position. But it doesn't have to be that way—not if you assume the initiative when in a buying position. Power negotiators like James Hardeman, purchasing agent for an electronics firm, use the tactic with a high degree of success.

ASSUMING AND KEEPING THE INITIATIVE

"One of the biggest mistakes buyers make," said Hardeman, "is in not being *prepared* for a major purchase like a car. You see, buying is really a lot like selling. It's merely the opposite side of the same coin. You rarely see a top professional salesperson go on a sales call without having a well-rehearsed game plan."

Hardeman's advice seems worth considering. Being a *professional* buyer, he must get the best possible deal for his company. And about the only way he can consistently get the best deal is to know everything he possibly can about the product he is buying and the person and company selling it.

What's the track record of the seller? Does he routinely live up to his commitments? Does he meet schedules? Does he have a reputation for dealing in good faith? Is the company's management strong? The purchasing agent needs the answers to these and other questions in order to negotiate successfully with sellers.

How About "Qualifying" Sellers

Obviously, the typical buyer doesn't have the purchasing agent's resources to conduct an in-depth research of the seller. Still, with a little digging, the typical buyer can usually gather enough facts on which to negotiate from a relatively strong position.

"The point is," Hardeman added, "a professional salesperson will invariably qualify his or her buyer. So why can't buyers 'qualify' sellers? They can, and in my opinion, should!"

Using Hardeman's Guidelines

Let's see how using Hardeman's guidelines might help you in buying a car.

First, it's advisable to shop around and narrow your choice down to one make and model—let's say a Ford tudor. Now make a list of things you want on the car, such as power steering and brakes, radio and cassette player, vinyl interior, and so forth. Now, armed with a clear idea of what you have in mind, go to a Ford dealer and ask what his bottom-line price will be—with or without a trade-in (and remember, the only relevant figure here is what your *net* cost will be and not what you are "allowed" for your old car).

Repeat this process with two other Ford dealers. In each case, make certain the dealer is quoting you a price based on the same model, with the same extras. Also, explain to the dealer that you are *comparing* prices and for this reason want his very best offer the first time around. This will tend to discourage the dealer's lowballing you.

Why the Tactic Works

I found that sellers generally dislike this approach for a couple of reasons. First, they resent your having shopped around. Second, it limits *their* negotiating powers. When car salesmen complain about such matters, I counter by saying, "Look, I really don't know much about cars. The only way I can tell if your offer is a good one is to compare it with somebody else's."

This will cause some dealers to give their best price. Others will hedge, saying something like, "This is my price, but check with me before you buy." I interpret this kind of remark to mean the dealer is still negotiating. Thus I belabor the fact that I plan to buy based on the price quoted *right now*!

There are several distinct advantages to the buyer's assuming the initiative when he can.

For starters, it allows the buyer to exercise considerable control over the negotiation interview. (And it's important to remember that typically, it's the salespeople who work very hard to gain and keep control.)

Getting a Realistic Price

Second, it precludes the buyer's having to choose between apples and oranges. This is almost always the case when a buyer is forced to choose between models with different features; or worse, between different car makers. In an earlier chapter, you'll recall, we mentioned how it was almost impossible for government buyers to choose between a prototype fighter proposed by General Dynamics and one proposed by Boeing. The decision was extremely difficult because they were comparing "features" with "cost," the old apples-and-oranges bit again.

Finally, by confronting the seller with solid facts, he reduces the chance of his being lowballed and maximizes his chances of being quoted a *realistic* sales price.

MAKING (AND REJECTING) PHONY OFFERS

There is still another way for a buyer to cope with a seller's lowballing tactic. He can use the same principle in reverse—a variation of the highballing tactic known as a *phony offer*.

For example, I recall this tactic being used successfully by a Fort Worth resident who was trying to buy a home from an individual seller. By buying from an individual, he figured he could "save the cost of the Realtor's commission."

The buyer found such an owner, who was moving out of town in "about a month." The owner was asking "in the neighborhood of $75,000." Quite certain that this was *the* house for him and his wife, the buyer offered the seller $77,000—$2,000 over the owner's ball-park figure. Naturally, the seller was delighted to close such a deal.

Buyer Puts Up $100 Earnest Money

The buyer gave the seller $100 down to "hold" the property, and promised to get back with the seller as soon as he made loan arrangements.

Two weeks went by without the seller hearing from the buyer. Meanwhile, of course, the seller had taken the property off the market and was not showing it. When nearly three weeks had elapsed without hearing from the buyer, the seller, now frantic at the prospect of having to move out of town without closing the deal, called the buyer and asked for an explanation.

"No real problem," the buyer explained. "The loan company has been dragging its heels, but we ought to hear something momentarily."

Buyer's Loan "Falls Through"

A few days later, the buyer called the seller back with some bad news. "I'm sorry," he explained, "the loan company won't give us a ninety-five percent loan as we had expected. We'll have to pay 10 percent down. And the only way we're going to be able to do that is to give you $70,000 for your house."

The seller's first angry reaction was to turn down the offer. But he reconsidered after pondering his limited options. If he rejected the $70,000 offer, he would have only one week in which to sell the property before moving—an almost impossible task unless he sold at an even lower price.

His other option was to list the property with a Realtor, then go ahead and move. But this way, he would have to pay a commission. What's more, he had heard a number of horror stories about what happened to other homes in the neighborhood that had been vandalized after owners moved and left them vacant. Considering all these factors, he reluctantly accepted the $70,000.

Using Phony Offer Judiciously

The *phony offer* tactic is an excellent way to get a seller over the barrel. The seller removes his goods or services from the market and more often than not, is willing to go ahead and sell at a lower price rather than go back through the whole sticky negotiating process.

For this very reason, the tactic should be used sparingly and with discretion. The question is more likely to be: How do you keep an unscrupulous or clever buyer from using the technique against you?

Question Buyer's Motive

Of most importance is the *motive* of any buyer who offers what appears to be too high a price for your goods or services.

There is a possibility the too-high offer is being made because the buyer is unaware of the going rate.

For example, real estate prices vary widely from one part of the country to another. In addition, real estate values are appreciating rapidly almost everywhere. Because of these conditions, a buyer *could* conceivably come in with too high an offer.

But such cases are probably the exception. You should *always* consider the possibility that a too-high offer is phony, and its main purpose is to get your product off the market. The tipoff in the foregoing case would have been the $77,000 offer, after the seller had given a ball-park figure of $75,000.

Insist on Large Down Payment

Beyond carefully analyzing the buyer's motive in making too high an offer, you should insist on terms which are likely to insure the success of your transaction.

For example, the seller in this instance should have insisted on a much higher down payment, or earnest-money check, to hold the property. On a $70,000 sale, it's not unreasonable to ask for a $2,500—or higher—earnest-money check to show good faith. Then if the buyer backs out, the seller at least has a good bit of cash to compensate him for his trouble. A $100 payment to hold a $70,000 purchase is almost laughable and should make the buyer's motive suspect.

Buyers Usually Start Low

Making offers that are too high, however, isn't likely to be the stock in trade of the power negotiator. He recognizes better than most that *buyers who start low and sellers who start high usually do better in negotiations*. Virtually all research in the field confirms this contention.

Power negotiators also recognize that where possible, they should get the other party to commit first when it comes to pricing. Buyers in particular should follow this principle most of the time, since it is the seller who is trying to market his wares or services. You'll recall, for example, that George Watson, the executive placement counsellor, advises his clients to let the employer name the starting salary rather than have the applicant state a desired price. The same would be true in asking a person who is selling his own home what he is asking.

ASKING SELLER TO SET PRICE

How does the seller's naming a price potentially benefit the buyer? Well, there is always the possibility, however remote, that the seller will *under*price his goods. It *does* happen occasionally, especially when the seller is unaware of escalating prices.

But more likely, the seller will put too high a price on his product. That's all right, too, since it gives the buyer some idea of where he can *start* negotiating. If the seller starts ridiculously high, he can start ridiculously low. If he starts moderately high, he can follow suit, and so forth.

Next time a seller asks you what you will give him for his product, you might reply, "Since you want to sell, and I might—or might not—want to buy, why don't you let me know what you want?"

"Out" and Back "In"

When other tactics fail, buyers like to play possum. It'll work every once in a while. Let's say, for example, that you are one of several people trying to buy a piece of commercial property. When the seller tells you what he is asking, you reply, "That's out of my league," and ostensibly drop out of the picture.

But let's further suppose that the property doesn't sell right away. You then return to the seller and say, quite confidentially, "Now that I'm out of the picture, tell me, what is the lowest price you would have accepted for that property?" Feeling you're no longer a prospect, the seller is likely to let his hair down and let you in on his selling strategy. And who knows, if the price is right, you might want to "revive" your interest in the bidding. This sort of thing happens.

USING A VARIETY OF POWER TACTICS

Many of the tactics and techniques we've discussed can be used at one time or another by buyers. However, a few of these—notably *buy-now-pay-later*, *last-and-final-offer*, and *association*—bear brief analysis.

DOD Buys for Future

To keep abreast of the times, the Department of Defense (DOD) must buy today for an uncertain future. The state of the art in aerospace continues to change at a dizzying pace. Thus DOD must buy now and promise to pick up the biggest part of the tab when the product is finished, usually some years downstream.

This type of negotiation is usually handled with a letter of intent. This document says DOD *intends* to buy the product after it is built, tested and proven combat ready. Meanwhile, DOD doles out just enough money to pay the manufacturer for development costs and purchase of long lead-time items.

Phrasing the Letter Carefully

Assuming the letter of intent is carefully written to cover all contingencies, such an arrangement gives the buyer several advantages. For example, a properly executed letter commits the DOD on a short-term rather than a long-term basis. This protects the buyer in several ways.

First, it absolves the DOD of future obligations in case the manufacturer is not able to produce the hardware satisfactorily and on time. Understandably, manufacturers do sometimes fall short in developing ultrasophisticated weaponery.

Obsolescence Is Major Problem

DOD also lives with the possibility that some of its futuristic products will become obsolete by the time—or even *before*—they roll off the assembly line. This has been true in development of aircraft. By the time many aircraft are built, flight tested and ready for production, the Air Force has already decided that it needs something bigger, better—and usually—faster.

The government spent many millions on the B-1 bomber before scrapping the project. Planners felt the B-1 was too expensive; further, they couldn't figure out exactly what its role would be *vis-a-vis* intercontinental missiles. The government spends a great deal on such projects. But they save a great deal, too, by buying now and promising to pay later.

CREDIT: A WAY OF LIFE

On a more personal basis, most Americans seem to thrive on the buy-now-pay-later principle. It's called credit, and its the backbone of our economy. Assuming one doesn't overextend it, credit is a sound way of living. And there are some advantages.

For example, I purchased a rather expensive television set from a local dealer. The set gave me all sorts of trouble. The dealer sent out a repairman at least a dozen times to try to pinpoint the problem. But to no avail!

What kind of negotiating leverage did I have in this situation? Practically none. My only recourse, which I eventually had to take, was to report the incident to the Better Business Bureau, which I eventually did. Only then did the dealer exchange my "lemon" television set for a new one. But look what it cost me: Considerable mental anguish, heightened blood pressure, and literally hours of lost time pursuing the action.

Postponing Cash Payment

Nowadays, I rarely pay cash for a major purchase, at least not at the time I'm buying. I try to buy with the idea of paying in full within 60 or 90 days, which most companies will allow interest free. If something goes wrong in that time frame, I have, *without exception*, been able to get prompt service. There's simply no doubt in my mind that buying now and paying later can give you negotiating strength.

LAST AND FINAL OFFER

A buyer and seller can sometimes negotiate indefinitely without either side making a major concession. Sometimes— and it depends entirely on the situation—a buyer can satisfactorily resolve this impasse with a last-and-final offer.

There are several factors, I think, which will determine how successfully the tactic will work.

Union-Management Reach Deadlock

1. *The buyer should have some indication that the seller will accept the offer.*

For example, I once witnessed a long and often heated negotiation between representatives of union and management. The main issue was a pay increase. The union felt it had justified a 15 percent increase; management "proved" it could not possibly afford more than a 10 percent increase.

When the negotiation reached an obvious dead end, management negotiators called a caucus. Shortly thereafter, the chief management negotiator announced categorically that under present economic conditions, the company could not possibly offer over 10 percent.

To my surprise, but apparently *not* the chief negotiator's, the union accepted the offer.

"Didn't you run a big risk," I asked the chief negotiator

later, "in telling the union that you couldn't—and in fact *wouldn't*—go above 10 percent? What if the union had held out for more? Wouldn't that have resulted in a costly strike?"

"No doubt it would have," the chief negotiator said; "but that's the calculated risk you take when you use this kind of strategy. However, I try to use the tactic only when I feel the final offer has at least a 50-50 chance of succeeding.

"Intelligence" Pays Off

"For instance, you just mentioned the strike would have been costly to us, and it *would* have been. But that's just the point. Our intelligence reports showed that while labor leaders favored a strike if necessary, most rank-and-file workers—and most of their families—did not. And this, in the final analysis, is why we figured our making a 'final' offer would work. This time, we were right."

The chief negotiator, like other top negotiators I have talked with, admits there is also a certain *feel* for when the last-and-final offer should be used. Significant in this situation, too, is the point that the chief negotiator's "guess" was really a solid assumption. He tested the assumption, and in this case it proved valid.

Softening Your Language

2. *The tactic is more likely to work if the buyer avoids the words, "last and final offer."*

How would you feel as a seller if the buyer said, "This is my last and final offer; take it or leave it."

However you felt about the economics of the offer, I'll wager your instinct would have been to tell the seller, perhaps in less than kindly terms, that he could "leave it." Why? Because the words are obviously intimidating, even threatening. You would have been admitting, in effect, "Okay, you win. I'll defer to your superior skill."

If there had been a third party involved on your side, you would have lost face by accepting. Not only your economic, but your psychological needs would have been scuttled. Remember, again, that everyone likes to win something from a negotiation—at a minimum, his self-esteem.

Other Approaches Suggested

My feeling is that the seller is much more inclined to go along with the buyer if the buyer can find some way to soften the phrase, "last and final offer," and there *are* several ways to do this.

For example, I remember one buyer whose negotiation with the seller reached what he felt was the final-offer stage. But instead of taking a hard take-it-or-leave-it stance, the buyer wrote out a check and handed it to the seller (and his wife). "Here's my check," he said. "If you think it over and decide not to accept it, please mail it back to me after the weekend."

Saving Face Important

This way the seller didn't have to "back down" in front of his wife (you'll recall from an earlier chapter the strong negative influence a third party can have on a negotiation). Indeed, this gives him time later to rationalize to his wife his reason for taking less than he had publicly said he would take.

Another softer way to phrase the take-it-or-leave-it tactic is to explain to the seller, "I would like very much to buy your product at the price you ask. However, this is all the money I can come up with."

You can no doubt come up with some equally diplomatic phraseology.

What If the Tactic Fails?

3. *Don't use the technique unless you're willing to pay the consequence.*

If the union had rejected management's final offer of a

10 percent pay hike, what would the consequence have been? Probably a costly strike. But just how costly? That's the question management had to answer before committing itself to a course of action.

This goes back again to the basic negotiating premise that your actions should be based on solid assumptions.

HOW BUYERS USE ASSOCIATION

There is strength in numbers. Two negotiators in any form generally carry more clout than an individual negotiator.

For example, expensive custom-built homes in affluent neighborhoods are often hard to price, mainly because there are few homes nearby with which to compare them.

Such was the case when a Dallas attorney tried to buy a home in a highly restricted area of the city. The seller quoted a $250,000 price tag, which seemed way out of line to the buyer.

Friend Is Convincing

Next day, the buyer returned with a friend of his, a retired builder who was familiar with the history of the neighborhood. As a result, he could cite actual building costs and selling prices on many homes in the area. His arguments were so convincing that the buyer was able to purchase the home shortly thereafter for just over $200,000.

Bringing in expert testimony in the form of consultants or various experts is par for the course in legal proceedings, labor-management talks, and virtually any complex negotiation involving issues requiring highly specialized knowledge.

On Using a Shill

Not all such association techniques are so ethical. I know a well-to-do antique collector, a dowager, who uses a "shill" to help establish the price of certain art objects. Actually, the shill happens to be a good friend and neighbor of the dowager. She also enjoys antiques but is not necessarily a collector.

When the dowager sees an antique that suits her fancy, she sends in her friend to establish a price. Without the slightest intention of buying, the friend will talk the seller down to the lowest price. Then she passes this invaluable information on to her friend, who now knows precisely where to start her negotiation.

Group Power Helps

The technique is especially helpful on rare antiques that are difficult to price. These art figures are usually as valuable as the buyer wants to make them.

Another form of association is "group power." Several citizens in a neighborhood form an association, with an eye to buying food, clothing and perhaps other things at a low price. The more members the association can enlist, the better price they are likely to get.

FINDING A PRICE ADVANTAGE

An astute buyer is always on the lookout for ways to negotiate a price advantage. Witness, for example:

- The student who got a big discount on his Volkswagen by agreeing to have ads painted on the side door.

- The man who got a large discount on a swimming pool by letting the salesman use his pool as a model to show potential customers.

- The home owner who got a sizable reduction by letting the contractor keep his sign in the yard a few extra months.

- The small businessman who paid far less for his small

computer by serving as the "model" for a new business system being developed by the seller.

- A public speaker who got a discount on his clothing by publicly "advertising" his clothier at his seminars.

And so forth.

Chapter 15

STAGING A FORMAL POWER NEGOTIATION

More formal negotiations, such as those between management and the union or two corporate entities, normally require extensive planning.

To be sure, effective planning needs to be part of any personal negotiation (and *all* negotiations involve the personal element).

However, the person responsible for a full-fledged team negotiation will need all the skills and tactical knowledge he uses in personal negotiations, *plus* an even higher degree of executive skills. These skills include mainly the ability to *plan, organize,* and *control* the efforts of his team. These executive skills must be brought to bear in:

- Identifying—and researching—the conflict, or problem.

- Picking the time and place for the meeting.

- Naming team members and establishing limits of authority.

- Establishing "ground rules."

- "Rehearsing" for the negotiation.

Let's take a look at each of these steps in some detail.

RESEARCHING THE PROBLEM

Identifying—and researching—the conflict or problem. This all-important step involves your getting the facts; defining the *real* problem; setting your negotiation goals, based on solid assumptions; and finally, planning your strategy, including possible areas of compromise.

Research in this sense means digging for the facts. In many instances, say an initial negotiation between two departments in a company, participants can usually gather all the information they will need in their own back yard, so to speak. In a more complex negotiation, research will be more involved, perhaps using many of the sources mentioned in Chapter 8. In still other negotiations, such as those between management and labor, virtually continuous research is required in order to build up a case.

Focusing on the Real Problem

Why is research so important? Because it will produce the facts which will help you identify the real problem. Defining the problem up front is critical. Many negotiations fail because the opposing parties never agree on what the real issue is. I have seen all-day sessions end in little more than meandering bull sessions, simply because the participants were not talking about the same problem. In this connection, take Dewey's word for it that "a problem well defined is half solved."

For example, take the negotiation that is about to occur between a Dallas-based clothing manufacturer and one of its divisions located in East Texas. The parent Dallas company, which customarily granted high autonomy to its divisions, found itself unable to meet an increasing nation-wide demand for certain "Texas-style" leather products, including fancy boots. Most of these products were being turned out by the East Texas division.

This increasing demand came about shortly after John

Haney took over as general manager of the parent company. John came from a competing manufacturer, where he handled sales and sales promotion. His new emphasis on these functions at the Texas company has paid off; the company is now unable to keep up with demand.

Al Baxter Insists on Quality

Al Baxter, Manager of the East Texas division, has been with the company for almost 30 years and is nearing retirement age. He started in the plant as a leather worker and worked his way steadily up through the ranks. He is generally conceded to be a highly skilled craftsman who insists on turning out top-quality work.

Further, Al is generally known to be a "company man." Thus his dilemma. If he tries to speed up production by cutting corners, the quality of his workmanship is almost certain to suffer. Yet if he doesn't, the company will find itself in the unenviable position of not being able to meet increasing demands for its products.

John feels just the opposite. He insists Al could meet new demands if he would only update his "antiquated production methods" and "think more positively." John, incidentally, is a graduate of Harvard Business School and takes what Al calls a "statistical approach" to running the business.

John and Al Head Teams

Al and John have been named leaders of the teams set up to resolve the issue, and this alignment creates potential problems in itself. For starters, there are pronounced personality and philosophical differences between the two. These differences will no doubt permeate the entire negotiation. But the real issue seems to be the problem of meeting new product demands without sacrificing the quality workmanship for which the company has become famous.

Since the negotiation entails complex personalities and issues, it has evolved into a formal meeting. Obviously, both sides have a great deal of homework to do. And assuming equal negotiating skills on either side, the team which does its homework best is likely to score most heavily.

Thus the negotiation moves into the second phase of identifying the problem—gathering all the facts available about the issues and personalities involved.

Sizing Up the Opposition

Negotiators normally play hunches in sizing up the opposition. But it rarely hurts to back up such intuition with facts. Both Al and John need to answer a lot of questions. How has the opponent handled himself in past negotiations? Does he tend to make first concessions? If so, how many and how big? What are some of his favorite negotiating tactics? Have any weaknesses surfaced in previous negotiations? How about strong points? Answering these and many other questions about the opponent's style might give you that competitive edge you'll need at the negotiating table.

"Know thyself." Taking stock of your own negotiating strengths and weaknesses is an integral part of planning. For example, if you are perceptive enough to recognize that you tend to "fly off the handle" easily and your opponent is known for his infinite *patience* in negotiation, you had best find a way to either modify your own behavior or plan some tactic which will break through your opponent's placid demeanor.

Looking Inside for Facts

However, it is the issues themselves in most complex negotiations that require most of your research time. Many, perhaps most, of the salient facts about these matters can be gathered internally.

John, for example, can gain virtually all the information he needs about the East Texas division operation from company records. He will no doubt call on various experts (a point we'll discuss more in detail momentarily) to gather this information for him. Similarly, Al has all the facts about his own operation, plus the intangibles gained from 30 years of experience. He will need to call on other resources to get information about the home office operation.

Answering Some Questions

Several key issues are likely to undergo heavy scrutiny in the negotiation. However, the pivotal issues seem to involve marketing and production techniques.

Both sides need to take a hard look at—and to answer—some penetrating questions. Is the company using generally accepted marketing techniques? Is the current demand a fad, or is it likely to sustain itself over the next few years? Is it possible to adopt a new marketing concept? If so, how would this new concept affect quality?

Production needs require equally hard analysis. Would it be possible to sustain a high quality of workmanship and at the same time speed up production? Should production facilities be more fully automated? Would such mechanization affect quality appreciably? Only an in-depth look can produce sensible answers to these thorny questions.

The negotiator who confronts his opponent without having gained at least tentative answers to such questions is courting trouble, and probably defeat.

Firsthand Facts Impress

Firsthand observation is frequently the best and most authoritative source. Getting information "straight from the horse's mouth," whether through personal interview, direct mail, or telephone conversation, can give your presentation that decisive, authoritative ring.

After gaining facts and pinpointing the problem, the next step is to lay the groundwork for your negotiating strategy by making *assumptions* about your opponent and the issues. These assumptions are really educated guesses, based primarily on information gained in your research.

Assumptions Come Naturally

Making assumptions should come fairly easy for you. It's something you do almost all of the time. For example, you *assume* the other driver will stop at a red light, and that he will turn left when he flashes his left-turn blinker.

On a more intellectual level, you make assumptions about people and their actions based on what you hear and see. For instance, what assumptions do you make from the following passage?

> Some years ago on a cold day in January, a 43-year-old man was made chief executive officer of his country. Flanking him at the ceremony was the outgoing executive, a man who had led his country's armed forces in a war that resulted in the defeat of the German nation. This 43-year-old man was a Roman Catholic. Who was he?

The logical assumption is that this was the late President John F. Kennedy. All evidence points in this direction. But as a matter of fact, the man was Adolph Hitler!

Checking Assumptions Out

The point of all this? Every assumption, no matter how valid it appears, should be checked out. For example, being a defensive driver (as you should be), you probably make sure the other driver stops totally at a red light before you move, even though your light is green.

Making assumptions about your opponent and the issues involved in a negotiation is only the initial step. Your assumptions become valid only after you've tested them in the crucible of negotiation.

Al Sizes Up John's Position

What basic assumptions could Al and John make at this juncture?

Al can logically assume that John is a high achiever driven by a strong desire to please shareholders and put his company on the map any way he can. He can logically infer from John's previous comments, and from his strong sales background, that he is going to press for greater production, even if it means sacrificing some quality.

Al determines further in his research that John has a tendency to let his temper flare during negotiations, and to *bluff* when he feels things aren't going his way. Perhaps he uses the "controlled anger" technique. Thus Al knows he must decide if John's anger is legitimate or contrived. Al has further discovered that John is not reluctant to use the *fait accompli* and *deadline* techniques.

John "Reads" Al

On the other hand, John has made several basic assumptions about Al. Above all, John has concluded from his research, Al is a company man who has fought his way up through the ranks. He would probably go to great lengths to conform to new ideas laid down by the parent company.

Based on this assumption alone, John figures he would have little trouble getting his way in the negotiation. Being a perceptive negotiator, however, he has become acutely aware of Al's obsession for quality work. After all, he learned the leather craft when products were virtually hand made. For Al to agree to lesser quality would mean a major compromise of his principles. The questions is, would he make such a compromise for the good of the company?

Establishing Basic Game Plans

Based on these tentative assumptions, all of which must be tested, the principals to the negotiation have made sizable strides in the preparation phase. It would behoove both sides to heed the words of Louis D. Brandeis, the famous jurist, who said that nine tenths of the serious controversies which arise in life result from misunderstanding, result from one man not knowing the fact which to the other man seems important, or otherwise failing to appreciate his point of view.

As a result of having done their home work and having made reasonable basic assumptions, John and Al are now ready to lay detailed plans for their negotiation. In setting down a game plan, most power negotiators establish general goals they hope to attain. Al's in this case is to hold the line on quality while improving production in other ways, perhaps by adding more people. John's objective, on the other hand, is to increase production, period! He is not overly concerned with how it gets done, including the sacrifice of quality.

Setting Areas of Compromise

Being reasonable men, however, both Al and John realize that compromise is the essence of negotiation. In a successful negotiation, you'll recall, everyone should benefit. Everyone should feel he's gained *something* from the negotiation. Otherwise, why negotiate at all?

In considering areas of possible compromise, negotiators likewise establish points they feel are *not* negotiable. There is a tendency for the opposition to accept such points, assuming they're not totally unreasonable, as sacrosanct.

Setting Nonnegotiable Items

For example, one of Al's nonnegotiable items was to insist on keeping the same curing time for leather. He had reason to believe John would insist on shortening the curing cycle in order to speed up production, thus his decision to make the item "nonnegotiable." John, on the other hand, would not agree to negotiating extension of delivery dates. Obviously, he had reason to expect Al would want to extend delivery dates to relieve the pressure on production. Extending this date would seriously hamper his ability to increase sales volume, he felt.

There are at least two potential advantages to laying down nonnegotiable guidelines. It signals that you are dead serious and won't budge on a particular issue. It also strongly implies that you are willing to compromise on most other points, and that, after all, is what negotiation is all about.

SELECTING A MEETING SITE

Picking the time and place for the meeting. The next step—setting an appropriate time and place for the meeting—can be a crucial one. Unfortunately, many otherwise effective negotiators fail to give this step proper consideration.

Time isn't particularly important, unless it creates a problem for one party or the other. For example, Al suggested a meeting for early spring. However, this is when John usually has his annual sales meeting, so he insisted on holding the meeting several weeks later.

An important point is to anticipate how long the meeting might last and thus avoid any date that might possibly put you into a time trap. For instance, a Houston commercial real estate dealer, anxious to close a deal with a New York client, invited the New Yorker down for a weekend meeting in his home, anticipating that he could "wrap up the deal" by early Sunday afternoon.

Complications arose, however, and the negotiation droned on until late Sunday afternoon. Suddenly the New Yorker found himself on top of his deadline for making his return flight.

Being Wary of Deadlines

Convinced from the outset of negotiations that his visitor wouldn't leave without consummating the transaction (an erroneous assumption as it turned out) the real estate dealer had to make last-minute concessions that he had not planned to make. But what was he to do? It was a case of either making the concession or probably losing the prospect.

In meeting a time limit, be especially wary of early deadlines or for that matter, *any* deadline. The question to ask is,

"Could the deadline possibly have a bearing on the negotiation?"

Evidence suggests that deadlines do indeed have an effect on negotiations. For example, many negotiations are concluded late Friday afternoon, just before the weekend. Many others are somehow settled just before the start of holidays, especially before Christmas and Thanksgiving.

Your Place or Mine?

Where should John and Al have their meeting? John's place? Al's place? Or perhaps a neutral site? There are pros and cons to each.

In sports it is generally conceded that there is a home-field advantage. Teams usually win more games at home than they lose. This is probably caused by many factors, not the least of which is favorable fan reaction.

Negotiators don't normally have "rooting sections," but they can point to some other potential advantages of negotiating in their own bailiwick, such as sleeping in their own bed and having all the facts virtually at their fingertips.

"Forgetting" a Report

Negotiating in the opposition's camp has some advantages, too. For example, assume that during a negotiation you're called on by your opponent to produce a critical report—one that would not do your cause any good. You can conveniently point out with feigned dismay that you "forgot to bring it along," and that you won't be able to get it during the negotiation.

Home Team More Aggressive

No doubt the home-field advantage is largely psychological. Research on the subject shows clearly that negotiating in your own territory is likely to increase your assertiveness. Visitors, on the other hand, tend to be less aggressive. And on occasion, they even act deferentially toward the "host."

This is especially true at the international level, where the notion of home-field "supremacy" has considerable precedent. For example, the old emperors of China accepted visitors to Peking as "supplicants bearing tribute." Obviously this position has softened somewhat in modern times; however, foreign dignitaries visiting China are still not given the status they are given in many other countries.

Korean Talks Longest

But what does ancient Chinese history have to do with modern power negotiating techniques? Plenty, if you study the tactics used by Communist negotiators during the Korean peace negotiations. These negotiations turned out to be the longest, and in many respects, the most costly the United States has been involved in.

At the outset, for example, the United Nations team insisted on holding negotiations on a neutral noncombatant ship at sea. This way, neither side would have a home-field advantage.

But in this case, as in several others we'll discuss in a moment, the Communists displayed the seemingly infinite patience and know-how which has branded them as formidable negotiators.

Communists Insist on 38th Parallel

Instead of meeting on a neutral ship at sea, the Communists insisted on holding the peace conference in the supposedly demilitarized zone along the 38th parallel. Apparently eager to get on with the actual negotiations, United Nations negotiators agreed. After all, they must have rationalized, the zone was *demilitarized*.

But of course it wasn't. Only after the conference got well underway did the United Nations team discover that the conference site was actually in a combat zone under Communist control.

UN Team Treated Like Visitors

Thus the United Nations negotiation team, led by Admiral C. Turner Joy, entered negotiations in a very unfair position; to a great degree, they actually came as visitors. In the Communists' eyes, the United Nations negotiating team entered proceedings as definite "losers," and they treated the United Nations team accordingly. In fact the situation got so bad that on several occasions, the United Nations negotiating team was actually hassled by Communist guards.

The moral here is obvious. When the other party insists on holding the meeting at his place, question why. In some cases, the other party is simply being hospitable. But there's a chance—and a good one if the negotiations are for high stakes—that the other party has an ulterior motive in wanting to meet on his home field.

ESTABLISHING AN AGENDA

Setting the Agenda. What items will be discussed in the negotiation? What issues will *not* be discussed? Roughly how much time should be allocated for various issues? Who will be permitted to discuss what? These and a host of other items should be dictated by a well-planned agenda.

In general, an agenda tells the negotiators what subjects will be discussed and in what *order*. Quite frequently, the order of topics can give one side or the other a decided advantage. This is called "stacking the agenda." The Communists used this tactic to great advantage in the Korean peace talks.

What Should Be Discussed First?

Normally, negotiators like to put first on the agenda an item that is relatively easy to agree on. This gets proceedings off on a positive note, and in some instances, paves the way for agreement on more controversial issues.

Conversely, putting a tough-to-resolve issue at the top of

the agenda can create an instant crisis. This is precisely what the Communist negotiators did in the Korean talks. They insisted on putting the meeting site as the first issue to resolve, and no other topic could be discussed until this item was taken care of. Further, the Communists insisted on a cease-fire until the site was determined. No doubt feeling these matters could be taken care of rather quickly, United Nations negotiators agreed.

Communists Go One-Up

But they were dead wrong. As history shows, the Communists not only won a home-field advantage, they gained a tremendous psychological advantage by negotiating the cease-fire. At the time, the United Nations troops had the Communists in full retreat. The prolonged lull in the fighting—all brought about, mind you, by shrewd negotiating—gave the Communists a respite from enemy military pressure. As a result, they were able to regroup and enter negotiations from a much stronger position.

As a prudent negotiator, you'll do well to remember that the agenda provides a logical, step-by-step plan for negotiations. Both you and your opponent should have a hand in setting a sensible and mutually agreeable list of subjects to discuss.

Setting the Pace

If your opponent wants to set the agenda, be on guard. He may be using the agenda as a ploy, as the Communists did, for his advantage. On the other hand, you might want to insist on a kickoff topic that will put you in the driver's seat in the negotiation right away.

Let's say, for example, that John strongly recommends "Determining ways to step up production methods" as the topic to be put first on the agenda. "Get the big issues handled first," he might tell Al "and the other items will take care of themselves."

Things might work out just as John anticipates. The subject he has suggested *is* the crucial issue at hand, and resolving it up front might pave the way for a highly successful negotiation. On the other hand, it could just as easily have the *opposite* effect. Since the subject is potentially volatile, the negotiations could come to a screeching halt before they really ever get started.

Selecting an "Easy" Topic

Though there is no set pattern for establishing an agenda, consensus seems to be that it's generally better to put what is relatively easy to resolve at the top of the list of topics to be discussed. For example, the negotiation between John and Al might be kicked off with relatively minor issues such as "Setting the date for another meeting," or "Inspecting financial reports."

All parties concerned are likely to agree on these "easy" topics, thus getting the negotiation off on the right track. A positive start usually helps develop the cooperative attitude so necessary to a give-and-take session. This cooperative attitude will be likely to help when negotiations get down to more controversial issues.

Many negotiators give far too little thought to arranging the agenda into a format designed to produce an orderly resolution of the problems. Others fail to question the motives of opponents who *insist* on placing certain issues at the top of the agenda—as the Communists did in stressing the meeting site.

In short, take time to set the agenda—don't accept one blindly. Guidelines for setting a sensible agenda include:

Agenda Guidelines Set

1. Set an agenda that provides a step-by-step procedure for solving the problems.

2. Don't accept another's agenda without seriously considering what it includes—and perhaps what it does *not* include.

3. Remember that an agenda is nothing more than a *plan for discussion*; it is not a binding contract. Allow for changes in the agenda if and when it becomes necessary.

ESTABLISHING GROUND RULES

Ground rules. When do sessions start and end? What about the seating arrangement? Is there to be a time limit? Will teams be allowed to call in experts? Will they be allowed to change negotiators during the proceedings? What about security?

These are some, but not all of the questions both parties to a negotiation will need to agree on *before* negotiations get under way. Failure to have a mutual understanding on such basic issues can cause serious problems, including a complete breakdown in negotiations.

Seating Needs Special Attention

The seating arrangement, for instance, seems at first to be a rather mundane detail and it most often is. For example, seating is usually arranged so every participant has roughly the same kind of seat, view, and access to his or her team leader. Ideally, every participant should have a full view of every other negotiator. If possible, the team leader should be given a commanding position which will allow him or her to communicate with members of both teams.

Again, be wary of opponents who insist on "special" seating arrangements. The Communists again demonstrated their guile at the Korean Peace Talks by demanding—and getting—a seating arrangement that was to their advantage.

Making Unusual Requests

The Communist team insisted that the United Nations team face north in the negotiation—a seemingly innocuous request. Only later did the United Nation team realize that, according to an old Oriental custom, the team facing north entered as a "loser."

Further, the Communists placed their short-statured chief negotiator in a chair that was considerably higher than Admiral Joy's. This enabled the chief Communist negotiator to tower a foot or so over Admiral Joy.

In addition, the Communists insisted on putting their flag six inches higher than the United Nations flags at the negotiating table. The United Nations team, of course, refused such a request and demanded that all flags be placed at the same level.

Equal Seating Desirable

All these conditions were eventually settled, but in the aggregate, the almost childish tactics took their toll. They threw United Nations negotiators off guard, delayed meaningful dialogue, and probably caused United Nations negotiators to make some minor concessions they hadn't planned to make.

If you want your negotiation to get off on the right foot, try to have opposing parties seated as equally as possible. For example, in an informal negotiation between a boss and his subordinate, the ideal arrangement is for the two to be seated side by side, or at a round table.

Research shows participants tend to be more cooperative in this arrangement. On the other hand, the classic arrangement of the boss seated on one side of a big mahogany desk and employee on the other, usually in a less comfortable and lower chair, is least likely to create a cooperative atmosphere. The desk becomes a psychological as well as a physical barrier to communication.

SELECTING A NEGOTIATING TEAM

The negotiating team. Like a good athletic team, an effective negotiating team needs strong leadership and a cohesive effort from team members. The best way to insure this effort is to select team members who are not only experts in their given areas, but boast certain personality traits.

These traits, according to researchers in the field, include practical intelligence, high verbal ability, and the perception to detect and cope with power. It doesn't hurt, either, if team members have a high tolerance for ambiguity and uncertainty.

Negotiator "Leaks" Information

The need to screen members carefully is reflected in an incident that took place in negotiations between a steel company and one of its major subcontractors. The company was trying to conceal the fact that it was about to have a top management shake-up, feeling this knowledge might give the opposition a competitive edge at the negotiating table. Naturally, the chief company negotiator insisted on his members keeping mum on the subject.

Halfway through the session, however, the company lawyer got into a heated verbal exchange over a minor issue with the subcontractor's chief negotiator. Tempers flared and the lawyer blurted out, "Look, it doesn't matter what we agree on here. Our new president will want to do it *his* way, anyway."

The company negotiator tried to convince the subcontractor that the lawyer's remark was without foundation, but the cat was out of the bag. Control in the negotiation switched to the subcontractor's side.

Such incidents will inevitably happen, even in the best planned sessions. However, setting definite guidelines as to each team member's role in the negotiation can go a long way toward eliminating such verbal blunders.

Team Play Important

One well-known chief negotiator for his organization has gone so far as to serve as the spokesman throughout the entire negotiation. His team members contribute only when he asks them to do so. And even then, they are given specific instructions as to how to respond. "It's definitely authoritarian," the negotiator said of his style, "but it does prevent team members from voicing their personal views. It forces them to pretty well stick to the party line.

"Negotiating is very much a team effort. Aside from expertise, the thing I look for most in a team member is that person's ability to subordinate his feelings and views to those of the group—most of the time."

Expertise, of course, is vital. For example, John and Al will no doubt have to select knowledgeable people from a number of areas for their negotiation. Either side will require "expert testimony" from production types. In addition, both are almost certain to need inputs from Sales, Advertising, Quality Control, Finance, Long-Range Planning, and perhaps even top management.

Captain Plays Key Role

The challenging job facing John and Al is to mold these diverse personalities into a cohesive unit. As team captains, their job is to define issues and problems, develop sound strategy, and make and test valid assumptions.

In addition, the team leader needs to have the limits of his authority clearly defined. Can he make a binding decision on the spot? Or must he get final approval from headquarters?

This matter of authority, as we've suggested before, can be a critical issue. Strategies can sometimes be built around it. Delegating complete authority can endow a chief negotiator with a high degree of power, which can be a dominant force in the proceedings. A negotiator with complete authority is much like a quarterback who calls his own plays. He can make binding decisions based on the *feel* he gets for the game as it progresses.

How Limited Authority Works

However, many veteran negotiators will tell you there are many times when having limited authority is expedient.

"Limited authority" means you must normally present your opponent's proposition—and frequently your own—to a higher authority for a final decision. In Al and John's case, the final decision will no doubt be handled by the board of directors.

What are the chief advantages of limited authority? Foremost perhaps is the fact that it enables you to *justify* transferring responsibility. For example, a negotiator with full power might propose to one with limited authority, "All right, I'll give you a full 10 percent discount if you can promise delivery in a month. Okay?" "Sounds great to me," the opponent says, "However, I'll have to check it out with my boss to make sure we can make that delivery on schedule."

What Are Alternatives?

Suddenly, the limited-authority leader has switched the negotiation to a higher level. His opponent is now, in effect, negotiating with an "invisible" entity—headquarters. Activity is suspended until headquarters hands down a decision.

What are the alternatives? If headquarters goes along with the proposal, everything's fine; the negotiation ends successfully for both parties. But if headquarters turns down the proposition, it's back to the negotiating table.

Notice, however, that the negotiator with limited authority has emerged unscathed. After all, *he* didn't reject the opposition's proposal, "headquarters" did. And more often than not, it will be the opponent's unenviable job to come up with a *new* solution to the problem.

Coping with Limited Authority

This matter of who has what authority, and precisely how much, should be determined before negotiations get under way. If you find out your opponent *does* have limited authority, you might try to offset this "advantage" in a couple of ways.

One way is to refuse to negotiate with the other person unless he is given full authority. Assuming this is not possible, make it clear that if higher authority overrules a settlement which you both work out, it is he—not you—who will have to come up with a new solution to the problem.

"Take Ten"—the Break

What about coffee breaks, recesses and caucuses? By all means, spell these matters out. Failure to do so can result in some strange happenings, as it did during the Korean peace talks.

In these sessions, it was understood that the side which proposed a meeting would be responsible for calling a recess. Accordingly, American General James B. Knapp, chief negotiator for the United Nations team, waited for four and a half hours for Major General Ri Choosun of North Korea to propose a recess. Not a word was spoken during this time. Finally, General Ri got up, walked out and drove away.

All told, the negotiation lasted 11 hours and 35 minutes—the longest such meeting in the peace talks. Because no provision had been made for it, neither side ate nor went to the rest room in that period.

Security Is Important

Security is another matter that needs to be covered in the preparation stage of negotiation. Surprise almost always plays a role in a negotiator's strategy, and it's hard to make your game plan work if your opponent has information that can help him anticipate your next move.

Industrial spying happens mostly in the movies. But it could happen in almost any negotiation. To guard against such a possibility, let team members know how high the stakes are and how costly a "slip of the lip" might be.

As a rule of thumb, whether the negotiation is a simple one between two individuals, or a complex one between two corporate entities, feed information to all parties on a need-to-know basis. This includes your own team members. Recall how the distraught lawyer inadvertently got his team in a jam.

Negotiating with Communists

As a result of his experience in Korea, Admiral Joy recommended certain guidelines to be followed in future negotiations with the Communists. In varying degrees, these principles can be applied to almost any negotiation, especially the call for "clear and rapid-thinking" negotiators.

- No American concession should be made without an equivalent Communist response.

- The American team should be staffed with clear and rapid-thinking negotiators of the highest quality.

- Americans must be ready to use threat of force and to implement such threat if necessary.

- Integrity on part of Communists should not be *assumed*.

- Conferences should be brief and conducted within preestablished time limits.

This is not bad advice for any negotiation.

REHEARSING FOR THE NEGOTIATION

Rehearsing. Now that you've carefully selected your negotiating team, clearly defined the key issues, and established fair ground rules, you're ready to take on the opposition. Right? Wrong. One important step remains: Practicing, or "dry running" your plan.

But how can you conduct a practice session without knowing what the opposition will say, and how they will react to your proposals? The best way is to have one or more highly knowledgeable people on your side to assume a "devil's advocate" role. They will be hypercritical of your plan and to try to find as many flaws in it as they possibly can.

Playing the "What If" Game

Your devil's advocate will essentially play a game of "what if." *What* do you do *if* your opponent does this? Or that? If your advocate is doing a good job, you'll no doubt have to revise some of your approaches and strategems.

Let's assume, for example, that you are John and you have requested some of your associates—those that know the issues best, you hope—to engage you in a mock negotiation.

John Recommends Solution

Part of your game plan is to suggest to Al during the negotiation that the East Texas division take two steps to help accelerate production.

The first step is a short-term remedy: Put on a second shift until production starts to meet demand. Phase two, a long-term proposition, would entail construction of a $100 million expansion to the East Texas plant. It would take roughly three years to complete the new building.

John planned both steps in great detail. He felt certain Al would go along with this master plan. This assumption was based primarily on his perception of Al's business philosophy, plus information he had gained from his intelligence sources.

Plan Is Tested

An aggressive and competent executive, John realized his plan was ambitious, but feasible. He was also shrewd enough to realize that before he could present the plan in a formal negotiation, he needed to "run it up the flagpole to see if it would fly"; in other words, to present it to his devil's advocate in a dry-run negotiation. He did so, telling his associates to be as tough on him as they could. In part here's how the conversation went:

John: Al, I can appreciate your concern over quality.

We've built our reputation over the years on fine workmanship.

Advocate: Those are my sentiments exactly.

John: Good. But you know, we've both got a big obligation to the company. Somehow we've got to see to it that we fill those backlogs of orders that keep stacking up.

Advocate: Well, yes, of course I agree. But it's gonna take a real effort.

John: Right. And I've got a plan that'll do the job for us.

Advocate: Oh, what's that?

John: To begin with, I think we can tool up for a second shift at your division within a matter of weeks. See on this chart . . . I think we can get tooled up and ready to go for just a little over $3 million.

Advocate: $3 million!

John: Yes. As you can see here, I've broken down costs on this chart.

Advocate: Yes, but . . .

John: Now hold on just a minute, Al. That's just the first part of my plan. In the second phase here . . . as you can see on this chart . . . I've outlined a plan for a big expansion of your division.

Advocate: Well, it looks great. But let's go back to your first idea . . . that second shift. We came up with the same idea, and we put the pencil to it. Our figures came out quite a bit higher.

John: Higher?

Advocate: Yes, we put a $5 million price tag on starting a second shift. You see, the problem with your figure is that it doesn't take into consideration the cost of hiring and training a work force.

John: I don't see that as being a problem.

Advocate: Well, according to our records, it is—or would be. I think this would just make a second shift impractical. It wouldn't be cost-effective.

Back to the Drawing Board

The conversation continued in this vein until the issue on start-up costs was resolved. Conclusion: John had indeed underestimated his costs, raising considerable doubt as to the validity of his proposal.

What if the devil's advocate hadn't been assigned the role of researching, then role playing the part of the opposition? More than likely, the issue would have been raised in the *real* negotiation, seriously hurting John's chances of getting his point across.

Preparation for a full-fledged negotiation is rarely complete without a dry run. It's the best possible way to determine if your game plan is workable.

REVIEWING THE CRUCIAL STEPS

Remember the crucial steps in planning for a formal negotiation.

- Identify—and research—the conflict, or problem.
- Pick the time and place for the meeting.
- Name team members and establish limits of authority.
- Establish ground rules.
- Rehearse for the negotiation.

That's the way power negotiators do it.

Index